THE LAST SUPPER ON THE MOON

THE OCEAN OF SPACE, THE MYSTERY OF GRACE,
AND THE LIFE JESUS DIED FOR YOU TO HAVE

STUDY GUIDE | FIVE SESSIONS

LEVI LUSKO

Harper*Christian*
Resources

The Last Supper on the Moon Study Guide
© 2021 by Levi Lusko

Requests for information should be addressed to:
HarperChristian Resources, 3900 Sparks Dr. SE, Grand Rapids, Michigan 49546

ISBN 978-0-310-13551-7 (softcover)
ISBN 978-0-310-13552-4 (ebook)

HarperChristian Resources titles may be purchased in bulk for church, business, fundraising,
or ministry use. For information, please e-mail ResourceSpecialist@ChurchSource.com.

Published in association with the literary agency of Wolgemuth & Associates.

Rocket schematics and small lunar module icon appearing on the session title pages were
created by Marcin Szpak.

First Printing November 2021 / Printed in the United States of America

THE LAST SUPPER ON THE MOON

The man read from a three-by-five index card he had taken from his pocket, on which the words of Jesus were written: "I am the vine; you are the branches. If you remain in me and I in you, you will bear much fruit; apart from me you can do nothing" [John 15:5]. Hands shaking, he took out a flask and poured the liquid into a chalice he had brought with him for this very occasion.

The wine glanced off the bottom and mysteriously curled up the edges of the glass. He paused, and then lifted it to his lips. The man opened another pouch, mindful of the paper-thin walls that were keeping him alive. He looked across the small, crowded compartment and saw the face of an amiable stranger. He lifted the bread, said a prayer, and ate alone. "This is my body, which is for you; do this in remembrance of me" [1 Corinthians 11:24].

The man's radio crackled to life. Snapping back to attention, he focused on the hundreds of switches and fuses covering every visible surface. He too had a mission. In just under two hours, he would leave the crowded space he was in and step into the ages. History had already been made.

His name was Buzz Aldrin, and he just had celebrated the Last Supper. The first meal ever eaten on the moon.[1]

CONTENTS

INTRODUCTION

The Apollo 11 moon landing that took place on July 24, 1969, is hands down the greatest thing that mankind has ever done. There has never been a more important feat of exploration than two humans traveling to the moon, landing on it, and then returning back home to planet earth. Landing on the moon was the result of a visionary president stunning his own space agency—and the world—with a promise that committed them to a project they did not have the ability to complete or the technology to accomplish at the time.

But while the moon landing may be the greatest thing that *mankind* has ever done, the cross is the greatest thing that has *ever* been done. There will never be a more important feat of *salvation* than God hanging on a cross. The fact that Jesus ended up there was the result of an all-loving God stunning the world with a plan to restore sinful humanity to him. Jesus' being lifted up on the launchpad of the cross was the biggest rescue mission in history.

As an avid fan of history, I am enamored by the parallels I find between Kennedy's mission to send a man to the moon and God's mission to send his Son to the earth. Just as I have been motivated to grasp what was accomplished in that impossible, against-all-odds, extraordinary chapter in our nation's history, so I have been motivated to grasp the *staggering* reality of what Jesus accomplished in humanity's history. It is my goal that as you go through this study, you will find this same kind of curiosity awakening in you as we explore everything that God has done for you through the cross and uncover what he has in store for you.

What took place at the cross can help you become grounded. What Jesus did in his body can help you become comfortable in yours. So come with me! We will travel in our imagination on a lunar voyage and believe God will give us grace to conquer that ever-elusive, easy-to-miss, often-ignored-but-never-silenced secret inner space.

Ten.

Nine.

Eight.

Eight point nine (ignition sequence start).

Seven.

Six.

Five.

Four.

Three.

Two (all engines running).

One.

Zero (liftoff).

And away we go.[2]

— Levi Lusko

HOW TO USE THIS GUIDE

The Last Supper on the Moon video study is designed to be experienced in a group setting (such as a Bible study, Sunday school class, or small group gathering) and also as an individual study. Each session begins with a welcome section, two questions to get you thinking about the topic, and brief reading from the Bible. You will then watch a video with Levi Lusko, which can be accessed via the streaming code found on the inside front cover.

If you are doing this study with a group, you will then engage in some directed discussion and close with a time of personal reflection and prayer. Each person in the group should have his or her own copy of this study guide, and you are also encouraged to have a copy of *The Last Supper on the Moon* book, as reading it alongside the curriculum will provide you with deeper insights. See the "For Next Week" section at the end of each between-studies section for the chapters in the book that corresponds to material you are discussing.

To get the most out of your group experience, keep the following points in mind. First, the real growth in this study will happen during your small-group time. This is where you will process the content of the teaching for the week, ask questions, and learn from others as you hear what God is doing in their lives. For this reason, it is important for you to be fully committed to the group and attend each session so you can build trust and rapport with the other members. If you choose to only go through the motions, or if you refrain from participating, there is a lesser chance you will find what you're looking for during this study.

Second, remember that the goal of your small group is to serve as a place where people can share, learn about God, and build intimacy and friendship. For this reason, seek to make your group a safe place. This means being honest about your thoughts and feelings and listening carefully to everyone else's opinion. (If you are a group leader, there are additional instructions and resources in the back of the book for leading a productive discussion group.)

Third, resist the temptation to fix a problem someone might be having or to correct his or her theology, as that's not the purpose of your small-group time. Also, keep everything your group shares confidential. This will foster a rewarding sense of community in your group and create a place where people can heal, be challenged, and grow spiritually.

Following your group time, reflect on the material you've covered by engaging in any or all of the between-sessions activities. For each session, you may wish to complete the personal study all in one sitting or spread it out over five days. Note that if you are unable to finish (or even start) your between-sessions personal study, you should still attend the group study video session. You are still wanted and welcome at the group even if you don't have your "homework" done.

Keep in mind the videos, discussion questions, and activities are simply meant to kick-start your imagination so you are open to what God wants you to hear and how he wants you to apply it. As you go through this study, listen to what he is saying to you and consider your own journey in light of what you learn about God's incredible plan to save you from your sin.

Sound good? Then let's get started!

Session One

CRISIS IN THE SKIES

We choose to go to the Moon in this
decade and do the other things, not
because they are easy, but because they
are hard . . . because that challenge is one
that we are willing to accept, one we are
unwilling to postpone, and one which we
intend to win,

President
John F. Kennedy

For God so loved the world that he gave
his one and only Son, that whoever
believes in him shall not perish but have
eternal life. For God did not send his Son
into the world to condemn the world, but
to save the world through him.

John 3:16–17

WELCOME

History forever changed on October 4, 1957, when the Soviet
Union successfully launched the satellite Sputnik I into
space. Although the spacecraft was only about the size of a

beachball, the impact it had on the American psyche was immense. This was the Cold War era—a time of tension between the nations—and it seemed to the Americans that the Russians were keeping one step ahead in the space race. The fear was that the Soviets would soon hold dominance in outer space and be able to rain down nuclear missiles at will on cities in the United States.

Clearly, something had to be done to tip the scales. The engineers in America's fledgling space program quickly got to work to solve the problem. But in the months that followed, it became apparent just how far the United States was behind Russia when it came to sending a craft into space. The nation's first attempt at a rocket launch on December 6, 1957, didn't even make it four feet into the air before it blew up. It was quickly dubbed "Flopnik."

President John F. Kennedy also recognized the crisis that Sputnik I presented. But his solution was nothing that anyone expected. Kennedy's bold plan was to *leapfrog* the Russians and win the space race outright by being the first nation to send a man to the moon and return him home safely. The problem was that when he announced this "moonshot," everyone at the space agency knew that almost none of the technology or infrastructure that would be needed to make it happen had yet been invented!

Kennedy was undeterred. "We set sail on this new sea," he said, "because there is to be new knowledge to be gained, and new rights to be won. . . . But why, some say, the Moon? Why choose this as our goal? . . . We choose to go to the Moon in this decade and to do the other things not because they are easy, but because they are hard; because that goal will serve to organize and measure the best of our energies and skills;

because that challenge is one we are willing to accept, one we are unwilling to postpone, and one which we intend to win."[3]

What President Kennedy proposed was ambitious. It was overwhelming and crazy. But as we will see in this first session, the same could be said of a different kind of mission that God announced in a "speech" back in the Garden of Eden. The world's first humans had just fallen prey to Satan's temptations and disobeyed God, ushering sin and death into the world. It was a crisis in the skies. But God had an ambitious plan for our salvation.

SHARE

If you or any of your group members are just getting to know one another, take a few minutes to introduce yourselves. Then, to kick things off, discuss one of the following questions:

- What comes to mind when you think of NASA and the space program?

— *or* —

- What stood out to you about this study and what do you hope to gain from it?

READ

Invite someone to read aloud the following passage. Listen for fresh insights as you hear the verses being read, and then discuss the questions that follow.

For God so loved the world that he gave his one and only Son, that whoever believes in him shall not perish but have eternal life. For God did not send his Son into the world to condemn the world, but to save the world through him. Whoever believes in him is not condemned, but whoever does not believe stands condemned already because they have not believed in the name of God's one and only Son. This is the verdict: Light has come into the world, but people loved darkness instead of light because their deeds were evil. Everyone who does evil hates the light, and will not come into the light for fear that their deeds will be exposed. But whoever lives by the truth comes into the light, so that it may be seen plainly that what they have done has been done in the sight of God.

JOHN 3:16–21

What does this passage say about Jesus' mission to this earth?

What is the promise that this passage offers for those who believe in what Christ has done?

W A T C H

Play the video segment for session one (see the streaming video access provided on the inside front cover). As you and your group watch, use the following outline to record any thoughts or concepts that stand out to you.

In 1961, President Kennedy delivered what would become known as the "moonshot speech." He said that America was going to take back the air and reclaim the high ground that is outer space.

But God's plan was even more complex, more crazy, and more audacious than John F. Kennedy's moonshot scheme. He chose to leapfrog past all the problems of sinful humanity by sending his Son, Jesus, to the earth to die on the cross, rise from the dead, and save us from our sins.

We've heard before that the cross is necessary for us to be forgiven from our sins. But we need to understand that the cross is also there to help us with our *secrets*.

The cross is not just a rescue mission to save us from our sins but also to help us see our secrets in a brand-new light—those parts of us that are just more interesting because they are damaged.

God gave us the gospel and sent his Son into the world to die for us. He now wants us to go out with that same message and work as one to restore the hope of a lost and fallen humanity.

There is a weight to sin. God allowed Jesus, his Son, to deal with that heavy weight of sin so that we would have the fear of death and have the pain taken off of us.

The Hebrew word for *forgiveness*—the Hebrew word that describes the weight of sin being taken away—is *nasa*. Our God is a God who forgives and takes away the weight of our sin.

Just as John F. Kennedy's plan changed the course of world history, so God's plan has changed the course of all eternity, giving us a possibility for life where previously there was only death.

D I S C U S S

Take a few minutes with your group members to discuss what you just watched and explore these concepts together.

1. America faced a "crisis in the skies" in the late 1950s. How would you describe that crisis? What was President Kennedy's bold solution to address the situation?

2. Read Ephesians 2:1–4. What is the "crisis in the skies" taking place in the spiritual realm? What was God's bold solution to address this situation?

3. Just like the moon, we all have a "dark side" that we try to keep hidden—those parts of us that have been damaged. Why do we tend to hide these parts from others?

4. Read 2 Corinthians 12:6–10. What does Paul say about his weaknesses? How have you seen God use a weakness in your life and turn it into a strength?

5. Read Exodus 34:6–7. What does God say about his character in these verses? How have you experienced the power of God's forgiveness in your life?

6. God can bring change in your past, your present, and your future. As you begin this study, in which of these areas would you most like to experience change?

RESPOND

Briefly review the outline for the video teaching and any notes you took. In the space below, write down the most significant point you took away from this session.

PRAY

One of the most important things you can do together in community is to pray for each other. This is not simply a closing prayer to end your group time but a portion of time to share prayer requests, review how God has answered past prayers, and actually pray for one another. As you close your time together, thank God for his bold rescue plan for humanity. Ask him to search your heart and forgive you for your sins. Confess your desire to find your identity in Jesus. And pray for God's love to saturate not just our world but the entire universe. Use the space below to write down any specific prayer requests or praises for the coming week.

Name   Request/Praise

_____   _____

_____   _____

_____   _____

_____   _____

_____   _____

_____   _____

BETWEEN-SESSIONS PERSONAL STUDY

The story of NASA and the Mercury, Gemini, and Apollo missions relates how the United States embarked on an ambitious plan to conquer outer space. But the mission that God sent Jesus to do in this world was even greater: to show us how we can conquer our inner space. An important part of this is studying God's Word each day. With this in mind, take some time to reflect on the material you covered this week by engaging in the following personal study. Each day offers a short reading adapted from *The Last Supper on the Moon*, along with a few reflection questions to take you deeper into the theme of this week's study. (You may want to review "Begin Here" and chapters 1 and 4.5 in the book before you begin.) Be sure to read the reflection questions and make a few notes in your guide about the experience. At the start of the next session, you will have a few minutes to share any insights you learned.

DAY ONE: THE PULL OF THE MOON

I feel the pull of the moon.

It speaks to me. Calls to me. Dares me to dream. Invites me to live fully.

Doesn't it control the tide?

When I look at the sky at night and see the moonlit wonder, the explosions of stars, I ask God, *How is it that you even notice me?*

Are its movements not somewhat hypnotic as it shrinks to a sliver and then grows full-size?

When I see it, I find myself calming down. I take a breath.

You sent us a companion to always be with us, reflecting the light of our sun in the darkness of night.

When I am afraid, I will trust in you and take great comfort from the night-light you left on for me.

When we lift our eyes and see the moon, we are connected to every human who has ever lived. Our lives look different than Abraham, Winston Churchill, Aretha Franklin, Chris Farley, George Washington Carver, Amelia Earhart, or Barak Obama. Yet when we look up to the moon in the night sky, we see exactly what they've seen.

Not just similar. The same.

We are not on Endor. There has only ever been one moon above our earth.

When I am stressed or scared, I like to look at the moon and remember those who have gone before me, and the fact that on many nights they probably looked up at the moon while they worried.

David's nauseous guilt over what he did to Uriah.

Peter's bitter sorrow over his denial of Christ.

The fear Esther felt as she prepared to step into the chamber of the king.

Daniel's agony as he defied the order and chose to pray anyway.

The problems they faced have come and gone, and the moon shines on. This is now your time to shine.[4]

David wrote that "the heavens declare the glory of God" (Psalm 19:1). What are your thoughts when you consider the moon and other aspects of God's creation?

Have you considered that when you lift your eyes to the moon, you see exactly what every other human has seen? What does that idea bring to your mind?

In Psalm 8:3–4, David asks: "When I consider your heavens, the work of your fingers, the moon and the stars, which you have set in place, what is mankind that you are mindful of them, human beings that you care for them?" How would you answer this question?

DAY TWO: THE MOON AS A BASE CAMP

Long after you and I leave this world, the moon will rise in the sky and shine. David called the moon God's "faithful witness in the sky" (Psalm 89:37). Its predictable orbit and nightly glowing points to the one who spoke it, hung it, and calls it out by name. He has a plan for you to shine in the midst of your struggles. Not some day when you sort out all your issues, or when you have a better job, or are out of school. Right now, in the middle of the suffocating smallness of your situation—he wants you to shine.

The moon is not an end but a beginning. Not long from the time of this writing, NASA plans to land on it once more—only this time it will not be as a destination, but in preparation. SpaceX was awarded the contract for the lander with their Starship, and the mission has been named Artemis—the sister of Apollo in Greek mythology.[5]

The moon is going to be a base camp for what lies beyond. When we land humans on Mars, it will be because the moon was a springboard for deep-space travel. This is what I hope this study can be for you: Artemis. A springboard. A base camp. Scaffolding.

Not an end but a beginning to a new way to be human. A fresh way to be you—as you were intended to be. Childlike but not childish. Without insecurity and toxic thoughts driving how you behave. With vulnerability and empathy. Tapped into kindness and selflessness. Noble, light, and free. Transparent, triumphant, and tender.[6]

Look up Psalm 89:37 and write it in the space below. What resonates the most with you as you read this verse?

Is it hard for you to believe God wants you to shine right now—right in the middle of your challenging situation? Why or why not?

How would you like this study to be a springboard for you? Be specific.

DAY THREE: THE DARK SIDE OF THE MOON

Did you know that we have only ever seen one side of the moon? Though it orbits around the earth, the same side faces toward us the whole time. It technically does rotate on its twenty-seven-day journey around our planet, but because it is tidally locked to the earth, it manages to do so keeping its rear away from us at all times.[7]

What is called "the far side of the moon" or "dark side of the moon" is always hidden. It is pocked by craters far more extreme than those on the side we see in the sky every night. One reason for this is obvious: as long as it has hung in the sky, the side pointing away from earth gets the brunt of any asteroids coming our way. I find it symbolic that the moon, like so many of us, keeps the most damaged (and interesting) side out of sight.

Aren't you exhausted from trying to keep the dark side of your moon safely hidden and out of sight? I'm not talking about putting your best foot forward. I'm talking about that hidden, horrible secret you have carried for so long: that there is something wrong with you. If people saw the real you, you think, they wouldn't want anything to do with you. So rather than being rejected, you pretend. But you don't have to. The craters and chasms and canyons of your character give texture and color and complexity that sparkle in your heavenly Father's eyes.

As you look full in Jesus' face, you will stop feeling the need to keep the comet-strewn darkness of your shadow side hidden from sight. You will discover that God is not afraid of what is behind you. He has a plan to address what is sinful, mend what is broken, and fill what is empty. He has a plan to use *all* of you—not just the curated parts you feel comfortable letting the world see, because—*news flash*—he already knows about the dark side of your moon.[8]

What is something that you keep hidden from everyone? What do you fear would happen if others discovered it?

God says that you are "a chosen people," "a royal priesthood," and his "special possession" (1 Peter 2:9). How does this tend to match up with how you see yourself?

How does Isaiah 61:1-3 address God's passion and power to completely heal and set you free—including the dark places with which you struggle?

DAY FOUR: UNDOING EDEN'S FAILURE

In the Garden of Gethsemane, Jesus was under such a crushing stress that he began to sweat drops of blood—a medical condition called *hematohidrosis*, where tiny capillaries near the sweat glands begin to burst. Undoing the failure of the garden of Eden, Jesus, the greater Adam, faced the crucible he had come for in this garden. The weight was that of ten million boulders being rolled across his soul. Imagine—flecks of blood mingling with sweat, causing his skin to glisten. It speaks of an agony that is unfathomable.

It was in that condition that he was arrested. Mocked. Chained. Punched in the face while blindfolded. Spit on. Handfuls of his beard ripped out. Remember, though he was God, he became fully man—and as a man could feel it all.

By the time he was ready to be paraded through town, the blood-soaked robe, which had dried, was torn off, reviving all the wounds that it had stuck to while it was worn. We know he was depleted and in no condition to carry the upper beam of his T-shaped cross, known as the patibulum, as was tradition on the nearly half-mile long journey through the old city to the hill called Calvary.[9] There he was crucified.

This all was so terrible that a word had to be invented just to describe its horrors. And so they did: *excruciating*.[10] A word that we toss around somewhat flippantly to describe a bad headache, or a time on pins and needles waiting to receive a call back after an interview. *Excruciating* actually means "from the cross."[11]

Read Genesis 3:1–7. What was the failure of the garden of Eden?

🌙 Read 1 John 3:8. What was Jesus' mission on this earth?

🌙 What did Jesus understand as he prayed in the garden about what he was going to experience in order to complete his mission?

DAY FIVE: A LAUNCHPAD FOR CHANGE

Isn't it so strange how you can't get away from the moon, try as you might, and yet you can't touch it? It remains perpetually in front of you as though you could stretch your arm out and grab it with your fingers, but it is just out of reach.

Happiness can feel like that. Like it is something other people experience but it only flirts with you and haunts you every time you glance out the window. You've tried everything, haven't you? You've read books and listened to sermons and gone through small groups and conferences. Something is still missing. Perhaps in all your investigation and accumulated information and revelation you sense that void. This study will help you with the piece that has always been missing, with core transformation—and that comes through exploration.

I want to show you that the cross has the ability to change you. It's a launchpad that will enable you to plant a flag on what otherwise remains unobtainable and unrelatable. Through this voyage you can expect true change in significant areas.

Your past. Not a single one of us can change history. Jesus can. He can forgive and redeem and restore what the locust has eaten and sin has stolen. And the harm others have piled on you? It can become fertilizer for the good he wants to produce through you.

Your future. He offers you the promise of a destiny. This future spills over into life after death. This will culminate in a new heaven and a new earth in which we will serve and explore into the ages.

Your present. I'm talking about participation in his work on the earth today. Plans he has been dreaming for you that begin today. Your mission awaits.

This is the fantastic quest to conquer inner space. I am here to tell you that enough time has been spent asleep. Your salvation is closer than when you first believed.[12]

When you look back at your *past*, what do you wish you could change? As impossible as it might seem, how might God use this past situation for good?

What dreams do you have for your *future*? How might this be part of the destiny that God has in store for you?

How do you see God at work in your life in the *present*? What do you need to do to align yourself with the opportunities that he is presenting to you right now?

For Next Week: Write down any insights or questions that you want to discuss at the next group meeting and review chapters 3, 4, and 6 in *The Last Supper on the Moon*.

PREPARE FOR LIFT OFF

I flew to the moon not so much to go there, but as part of developing the system that would allow it to happen.	Astronaut Neil Armstrong
Let us throw off everything that hinders and the sin that so easily entangles. And let us run with perseverance the race marked out for us.	Hebrews 12:1

WELCOME

When President Kennedy made his historic announcement to put a man on the moon by 1969, and return him home safely back to earth, the total time an American had spent in space was barely *fifteen minutes*. The feat had been accomplished on May 5, 1961, by Alan Shepard, a military test pilot, in a craft called *Freedom 7*. The launch had been televised and witnessed by millions.

In the aftermath of Kennedy's bold announcement, the leadership at NASA scrambled to put programs in place to meet his goal. It was determined that everything would be done with the aim of preserving American lives, so everything would be done slowly, cautiously, and in stages. Step one was to launch the Mercury program, with the goal of sending a man into space (accomplished by Shephard). Step two was the Gemini program, launched in 1965, with the goal of testing an astronaut's ability to fly long-duration missions. Step three was the Apollo program, launched in 1967, with the aim of landing a human on the moon.

It took NASA ten years to go from the failure of Vanguard (which the press dubbed the "Flopnik" or "Kaputnik") to the Apollo program. Ten *long* years of hard work, perseverance, and preparation to be ready for "lift off." Yet this pales in comparison to the *thirty* years that Jesus spent preparing to fulfill his mission. Or, for that matter, the *thousands* of years that passed from the time God announced the plan of sending a Messiah to the time Jesus was born. And when the time *was* finally right for Jesus to begin his ministry, the Holy Spirit led him into the wilderness, where he went through *forty days* of trial and testing to prepare him for the work ahead.

God works according to his own timetable and will send us through days, months, or even years of "wilderness" times to prepare us for the mission he has for us. When we look at our lives, we may see pieces and parts and things not fitting together as we think they should. We may think we are not moving at all—that our perseverance doesn't matter. But we can be certain that God is moving us forward . . . one small step at a time.

SHARE

If you or any of your group members are just getting to know one another, take a few minutes to introduce yourselves and share any insights you have from last week's personal study. Then, to kick things off, discuss one of the following questions:

- Why do you think it was important for NASA to reach President Kennedy's goal of sending a human to the moon in calculated stages?

— *or* —

- Why do you think both preparation and perseverance are needed to accomplish great missions? How do these two traits work together?

READ

Invite someone to read aloud the following passage. Listen for fresh insights as you hear the verses being read, and then discuss the questions that follow.

Do you not know that in a race all the runners run, but only one gets the prize? Run in such a way as to get the prize. Everyone who competes in the games goes into strict training. They do it to get a crown that will not last, but we do it to get a crown that will last forever. Therefore I do not run like someone running aimlessly; I do not fight like a boxer beating the air. No, I strike a blow to my body and make it

*my slave so that after I have preached to others, I myself will
not be disqualified for the prize.*

1 CORINTHIANS 9:24–27

What does Paul say our goal should be when it comes to the
Christian life?

Why is it critical to have both focus and perseverance in
following Christ?

WATCH

Play the video segment for session two (see the streaming
video access provided on the inside front cover). As you and
your group watch, use the following outline to record any
thoughts or concepts that stand out to you.

NASA's Mercury missions were to prove that we could get a human
into space. The Gemini missions were to test if two vessels could
rendezvous in orbit and dock back together. All these missions had

to be proven, perfected, and tweaked before the Apollo missions could even be attempted.

Similarly, when we read about God sending Jesus into this world on his rescue mission, we find that Christ was on the earth for the first thirty years without doing anything that we know about. It took a number of years before we reach what Paul says is "the fullness of time" (see Galatians 4:4)

Everybody assumed that when the Messiah came, he would be a great political ruler who would crush the Roman Empire and free Israel from captivity. But Jesus comes as a baby.

Joseph and Mary gave the offering of the turtle doves at the temple before God supplied the chest of gold. Even the Christmas song will tell you that two turtle doves come before five golden rings. Translation: they had to step out in faith before they could watch God provide for them.

The story of Jesus being found in the temple at twelve years of age reinforces that he had developed a regular habit or regular routine of daily putting God's Word into his heart.

In the Gospels, we find that Jesus had a way of sneaking off to spend time with God and get a little bit of Scripture into his heart. Could it be you need a routine of putting some positivity into your heart?

Jesus passed the tests in the wilderness when tempted and successfully did what Adam and Eve, our first parents, had not been able to do. The time alone that Jesus spent with the Father, and the time of preparation in Scripture and in prayer, gave him the strength to do the things that he did.

Have you put a morning routine into place where you are spending time with God every day? Are you in a small group of other Christians where you can be vulnerable? Are you plugged into a local church so you can deny yourself, pick up your cross, and follow Jesus along with his other disciples?

DISCUSS

Take a few minutes with your group members to discuss what you just watched and explore these concepts together.

1. The astronauts had to trust NASA's timetable for their mission. How is this the same when it comes to trusting in God's timetable for our lives?

2. Mary and Joseph offered a sacrifice of doves at the temple before they were supplied with gold from the magi. Have you ever stepped out in faith like this before you saw God provide for you? What was the situation? What happened?

3. Preparation and perseverance were key aspects of NASA's success in landing humans on the moon. Which comes easier for you—preparation or perseverance? Why?

4. One of the few details that we know about Jesus' life from around age twelve to age thirty is simply that he "grew in wisdom and stature, and in favor with God and man" (Luke 2:52). How does this verse reveal the ways that Jesus prepared for his mission?

5. Jesus told his followers, "Whoever does not carry their cross and follow me cannot be my disciple" (Luke 14:27). What was Jesus conveying to us about perseverance?

6. Great missions always come at great cost. What has following Jesus cost you—whether financial, relational, or in some other way?

RESPOND

Briefly review the outline for the video teaching and any notes you took. In the space below, write down the most significant takeaway from this session.

PRAY

As you close your time together, confess that God's timetable is always best and ask him to give you patience to wait on his timing. Pray that he will help you prepare and persevere for the tasks he has given you. And thank him for including you in his mission for the world. Use the space below to record any specific prayer requests or praises for the coming week.

Name   Request/Praise

_____   _____

_____   _____

_____   _____

_____   _____

_____   _____

_____   _____

_____   _____

BETWEEN-SESSIONS PERSONAL STUDY

Reflect on the material you covered during this week's group time by engaging in any or all of the following between-session activities. Be sure to read the reflection questions and make a few notes in your guide about the experience. At the start of your next group session, you will have a few minutes to share any insights that you learned.

DAY ONE: CRAWL BEFORE YOU FLY

How do you get a spaceship to the launchpad? Especially when that spaceship is 636 feet tall? That was the problem when humans went to the moon. They had to get the Saturn V rocket from the Vehicle Assembly Building to Complex 39A—a distance of 3.5 miles.[13]

To solve the problem, NASA invented something almost as impressive as the rocket it was built to carry: the Crawler. The rocket was built on this machine, which then drove the rocket and its tower vertically to the launchpad, where it could be fueled and then launched. The flat top of the original crawler measured 14,934 square feet, which was bigger than a baseball diamond.[14] When it was built, it was the largest land vehicle ever made by humans.

Why am I telling you all this? Because you can't get to space if you can't even make it to the launchpad. This might seem like overkill but know this: there was no other way. The Crawler transported the most complicated, powerful engine built up until that point by humans—the Saturn V rocket. And it carried it slowly. Very, very slowly.

The irony is that on the lunar missions, the astronauts would reach a top speed of 25,000 miles per hour, but they did so in a vessel that made its journey to the launchpad at less than a mile per hour.[15] That is one foot per second.[16] The rocket would shake the ground on its way out of this world, but it got to the launchpad at a snail-like crawl. This is why you and I need to be patient with ourselves as we grow. You gotta crawl before you can fly.[17]

Paul writes, "Let us not become weary in doing good, for at the proper time we will reap a harvest if we do not give up" (Galatians 6:9). What does this say about the importance of patience and perseverance when it comes to following after Christ?

🌑 Read Psalm 27:14. What does it mean for you to "wait for the Lord"?

🌑 When are some times that you have rushed and moved ahead of God's timing? What happened as a result?

DAY TWO: SACRIFICE BEFORE BEING SUPPLIED

I imagine money concerns were on Mary and Joseph's minds after they took Jesus to be presented in the temple. It's not as if they were loaded. They had just paid taxes, and there was the expense of the trip and the doves for the sacrifice. How were they to make this work?

Then the doorbell rang. (Yes, I know they didn't have doorbells back in those days, but just stick with me.) Mary and Joseph opened the door, and there on their stoop were three men. (We assume there were three because of the three gifts given, though it could have been more.) These three "kings" or "wise men" from the East gave gifts. Frankincense and myrrh (whatever those things are) and a gift we do understand: *gold*. Cash money.

With their visit came some advice: Herod is *loco en la cabeza* and means murder for the child. Don't stay here. Get out of Dodge. The gift of gold funded the expedition. It's remarkable that the three kings were most likely already on the road when Joseph and Mary were dipping into their emergency fund to pay for the turtledoves. God must have smiled as he saw their faithfulness, knowing the resources were already on the way.

I think that this is what the apostle Paul meant when he told the Corinthians that as they gave out of their lack, God would make all grace abound toward them (see 2 Corinthians 9:8–15). The vital point to not miss: the two turtledoves came before the five golden rings. Mary and Joseph sacrificed before they were supplied.

So it always is. We must step out in faith before we will watch God miraculously work in our lives. Our biggest problem is not ability or resources; it's often our imagination. We need the jolt this exploration of outer space will give us so we can wake up our wonder. Because if the moon does anything, it cordially invites us to a life full of imagination and exploration.[18]

Joseph and Mary sacrificed before they were supplied. What is a time in your life that you stepped out in faith? How did God provide?

Read 2 Corinthians 9:8–15. Why do you think God invites us to sacrifice and give before he supplies for our needs? What is he attempting to teach us?

🙂 Do you agree that our biggest problem is not our ability
or our resources but our imagination? Why or why not?

DAY THREE: THE GOSPEL'S EXCLUSIVITY

I've always had a problem with the story told in Genesis 22
of Abraham being willing to sacrifice his son. Something
doesn't sit right. We are supposed to applaud the faith of a
man who was willing to do such a thing? It sounded pretty
sick to me—until I learned that the culture of child sacrifice
saturated the people he lived among. A god requiring the
blood of a son was normative. What wasn't normal was God
telling him *not* to sacrifice Isaac.

Instead, the Lord promised that he would send his Son.
"Look, the Lamb of God, who takes away the sin of the
world!" (John 1:29). These words were spoken by John the
Baptist, answering the question that Isaac had asked thousands of years before: "Where is the lamb for the burnt offering?" (Genesis 22:7). Because of the forbidden fruit the first
Adam took from the tree, Jesus—the greater Adam (see Romans 5:15-17)—had come to die on one.

Some people take offense at the gospel's exclusivity in
stating that only one road leads to God. They feel that people
shouldn't be banished to hell because they picked another
team. Let me suggest a different way of looking at it. If you
were drowning in the ocean and someone saw you and came
to your rescue, would you bristle that only one option was
presented to you?

Let me humbly suggest that there is only one name that can. When you were lost in your sins, only one person was willing to come and die to set you free and give you life spiritually. Instead of protesting that there is only one way to God, celebrate that there is a way to God at all. Jesus is that way. Be rescued.

He descended from heaven to earth—and not just so you could go to heaven when you die. He did it so you could be raised to newness of life here on this earth (first spiritually and ultimately physically, but, between now and then, mentally and emotionally). He came so you could be witnesses of and party to his bringing heaven back to this earth as he resurrects and restores all things to himself by the power of the cross.[19]

Read John 14:5–7. What does Jesus say about himself in this passage?

Why do you think the gospel's message of exclusivity—that Jesus is the only way to be saved—tends to be offensive to people?

Read 1 John 1:9. Jesus doesn't just save us from our sins but also restores us and leads us into righteousness. What is he restoring in you right now?

DAY FOUR: LAUNCHED INTO A NEW LIFE

As we previously discussed, in Exodus 34:7, God describes himself as forgiving. The Hebrew word translated for "forgiving" is *nasa,* which means "to lift, carry, take."[20]

Jesus was lifted up on the cross in order to carry our sins and take them away so we could be launched into a whole new life. One in which you are forgiven but also in which you could become forgiving. This is why Jesus tells us in Matthew 6:12 to pray, "Forgive us our debts, as we also have forgiven our debtors."

To not release debts hurts you. And what you hold on to doesn't have to be something huge to be lethal. It's the little splinters of unforgiveness that are the most annoying, and if they become infected, they can cause big problems.

For you and me, we're triggered by things that are less like someone cutting off our heads and more like someone cutting us off on the highway. Not so much being stoned by a mob but political arguments over holiday dinners. Left unchecked, like a cancerous infestation, these roots of bitterness multiply, spread, and eventually kill relationships.

Fortunately, the forgiveness that works in big issues also works in small ones. And when you keep your eyes on the cross, mountains turn back into molehills.

To be an unforgiving Christian is an oxymoron. Like *jumbo shrimp, Icy Hot, mutual differences, only choice,* or a *tiny elephant.* We are, after all, the followers of Jesus—a man who used his dying breath to ask forgiveness for those who killed him. A Christian is both someone who is *forgiven* and *forgiving.* Everywhere we go we ought to show love.

I encourage you to pray this prayer: *Father, thank you for being willing to forgive me. I pray that, by your power in me, you would allow love and grace not to get stuck in me but to flow through me. Help me be not just forgiven but also forgiving. Amen.*[21]

Read Mark 11:22–25. Why is it important for us to forgive others?

Paul writes, "[Forgive] each other, just as in Christ God forgave you" (Ephesians 4:32). How can considering how God has forgiven you help you to forgive others?

What grudge do you need to let go of today? How would it feel to do so?

DAY FIVE: REMEMBER, REPENT, RETURN

We never drift in a positive direction. You don't doze off while heading to work and accidentally find yourself in the company parking lot. You end up in a ditch or an ambulance—or worse. Drifting doesn't take you to where you want to go; it takes you away from it. Thankfully, there's a surefire, three-step way to get back on course: *remember, repent, return.*

Remember. Remember what God went through to reach you. That the Spirit hunted you. That your grandmother prayed for you. Most of all, remember that Jesus died for you. There's a reason that the Last Supper is a call to remember. To go back. To feel it all over again.

Repent. Change your mind. Do a U-turn. Flip the switch. Make the conscious choice to not leave Jesus out of the things you do for God. This doesn't mean that you don't serve others. You just don't miss out on the opportunity to sit at Jesus' feet before you start serving.

Return. Go back to what you did at the beginning, when you were first amazed by God's grace. When you spent time with Jesus every day and talked to him like he was right there in the room. Time spent together is powerful medicine in any relationship.

You can come alive in a genuine relationship with God that will turn all the dull and dead spiritual activity into on-fire reality. Your relationship with Jesus can be pulsating, heartfelt, raw, vibrant, and full of joy. Leaping and whirling like David before the ark, totally alive.

Author and theologian C.S. Lewis called the Trinity "a kind of dance."[22] Your relationship with God is meant to be you joining that dance. Jumping to salute. Hopping for joy. Happy to be alive and not dead. You were not a person of God; now you *are* a person of God! You were *not* a child of the King; now *you* are a child of the king! Today is the day to remember, repent, and return.[23]

Read Ephesians 2:8–9. What is helpful for you to remember about your salvation?

Read Acts 3:19. What is the promise for those who repent of their sins?

Read James 4:8. What spiritual disciplines do you need to return to doing?

For Next Week: Write down any insights or questions that you want to discuss at the next group meeting and review chapters 7, 9, and 12 in *The Last Supper on the Moon.*

OBSTACLES IN ORBIT

We knew it was going to be difficult to get to the moon. We didn't know how difficult.

Astronaut
Alan Bean

In this world you will have trouble. But take heart! I have overcome the world.

John 16:33

WELCOME

NASA had now begun the Apollo program—the missions that would be aimed at sending humans to the moon and returning them safely home again. But the first mission resulted in tragedy. During a preflight test for Apollo 1, a fire broke out in the command module that claimed the lives of three astronauts. The men were asphyxiated when they were unable to escape through the hatch.

The fate of the agency was now in doubt. What many believed saved NASA was a speech given by Gene Kranz, director of flight operations for Apollo, in which he admitted to the agency's mistakes and vowed to never compromise again.

After a two-year hiatus, the Apollo program was started up again in 1968—a bit wiser now and a bit more cautious.

NASA ultimately designated Apollo 11 to be the mission that would land a man on the moon. Neil Armstrong and Buzz Aldrin would have the distinction of manning the lunar module, while Michael Collins remained behind in the capsule. But the descent to the surface of the moon would not be without its challenges. A "1202" alarm sounded at 40,000 feet. When that issue was resolved, the astronauts discovered another major problem. The lander was moving faster than expected and would overshoot the designated landing site on the surface.

Neil took control to steer past the unlandable terrain. But the extra flight time caused them to burn through extra fuel. As they came in for final approach, they had only sixty seconds of fuel left. In the end, according to Buzz, they had just fifteen seconds of fuel remaining in the tank before they would have had no choice but to abort the mission.

There were many challenges for the NASA astronauts to overcome. The same will be true in your life as a Christian. Sometimes the obstacles will come from outside sources. Sometimes the obstacles will come from within. Sometimes it will feel like you are navigating rocky terrain . . . and your fuel is running low.

God's promise to us is that if we keep following him, he will guide us through all of the obstacles in our path. He will provide us with perseverance and wisdom to endure the outside forces. He will give us forgiveness and restoration when the failures are caused by our own doing. He will be our "ground control" and will guide us through every problem at each step along the way.

S H A R E

Begin your group time by inviting those in the group to share their insights from last week's personal study. Then, to kick things off, discuss one of the following questions:

- How do you tend to respond when setbacks or obstacles get in the way of your plans? Has this response proven helpful over time?

— *or* —

- What are some of the important lessons that you have learned because of the setbacks you have experienced in life?

R E A D

Invite someone to read aloud the following passage. Listen for fresh insights as you hear the verses being read, and then discuss the questions that follow.

Dear friends, do not be surprised at the fiery ordeal that has come on you to test you, as though something strange were happening to you. But rejoice inasmuch as you participate in the sufferings of Christ, so that you may be overjoyed when his glory is revealed. If you are insulted because of the name of Christ, you are blessed, for the Spirit of glory and of God rests on you. If you suffer, it should not be as a murderer or thief or any other kind of criminal, or even as a meddler. However, if you suffer as a Christian, do not be ashamed, but praise God that you bear that name. For it is time for judgment to begin with God's household; and if it begins with us, what will the outcome be for those who do not obey the gospel of God? And,

> *"If it is hard for the righteous to be saved,*
>   *what will become of the ungodly and the sinner?"*

So then, those who suffer according to God's will should commit themselves to their faithful Creator and continue to do good.
1 PETER 4:12–19

How does Peter say we should view the trials we encounter?

What does it mean to "participate in the sufferings of Christ"?

WATCH

Play the video segment for session three (see the streaming video access provided on the inside front cover). As you and your group watch, use the following outline to record any thoughts or concepts that stand out to you.

One of the biggest hurdles in NASA's quest to send a mission to the moon was the death of three astronauts on the launchpad on January 27, 1967. But it was by no means the only hurdle. When Neil and Buzz were descending to the moon, the mission was almost called off due to a 1202 program alarm.

The world can seem simple compared to the complexities of navigating our own personal turmoil. God's promise is to guide us each step of the way through this exploration—this journey to conquer inner space—as we learn to embrace the dark sides of our moon.

The Jewish leaders should have been the ones to welcome Jesus. Instead, they set up obstacles to block his mission and to trap him, often challenging him in front of the disciples and the public at large. Their spiritual blindness would ultimately lead them to plot how to put Jesus to death on the cross.

The apostle Paul experienced betrayals, beatings, shipwrecks, and things worse than anything we've faced on a daily basis. Yet he knew that God was using those trials to unlock new levels of character and trust and ability within him. The hard times—and this isn't cliché—were truly making him stronger.

On a smaller planet, the mass and the attraction of gravity is different than on a larger one. The weight of something depends on where you're standing. In the same way, standing on God's promises can impact the way that we "feel" trials. A big trial feels lighter when you are anchored on God's Word.

Astronauts have to be constantly vigilant because they know there are many different things that can go wrong in space that can be fatal. Likewise, as we follow Jesus, we have to be vigilant. Not only because of those kinds of trials—the hard times, the heavy times—that we face, but also because of temptation.

It's easy to go through a hard time or a time of temptation, wipe your brow, say "phew," and let your guard down. But that is when you will not be ready for the next round of attacks that are coming.

The enemy is going to place challenges in our path to following Christ. So, let's not be shaken by those things. Let's not be surprised by them. Let's be expecting them. Let's have a plan for them.

DISCUSS

Take a few minutes with your group members to discuss what you just watched and explore these concepts together.

1. How do you think the astronauts' planning and training prepared them for the obstacles they would face in the moon landing? How does this kind of planning and training translate to the Christian life?

2. Which of the hurdles the Apollo astronauts overcame stand out to you most? Why?

3. Have you ever felt "fifteen seconds" away from giving up on something important when, suddenly, everything came together? What happened to turn it around?

4. Read James 1:2–5. What are some of the benefits that you have received after going through a time of testing? How does testing develop our character?

5. The astronauts knew that they could rely on the command center back in Houston for guidance, but they still had to stay focused on their mission. What does 1 Peter 5:8 say about how we must likewise remain vigilant in our trials?

6. When we fail in our trails, God remains faithful to forgive us and redeem us. How did Jesus prove this definitively on the cross?

RESPOND

Briefly review the outline for the video teaching and any notes you took. In the space below, write down the most significant takeaway from this session.

PRAY

As you close your time together, proclaim that there is no obstacle that is too big for God. Ask the Lord to give you the wisdom and strength you need to overcome your struggles. Thank Jesus for his faithfulness to forgive your sins. Remember how much can change in fifteen seconds—and ask God for the courage to not put off what you need to do now. Use the space below to record any specific prayer requests or praises for the coming week.

Name   Request/Praise

_____ _____

_____ _____

_____ _____

_____ _____

_____ _____

_____ _____

_____ _____

_____ _____

_____ _____

_____ _____

BETWEEN-SESSIONS PERSONAL STUDY

Reflect on the material you covered during this week's group time by engaging in any or all of the following between-session activities. Be sure to read the reflection questions and make a few notes in your guide about the experience. At the start of your next group session, you will have a few minutes to share any insights that you learned.

DAY ONE: FIFTEEN SECONDS

Neil Armstrong and Buzz Aldrin were making the final descent to the moon in the Apollo 11 lunar module, which they called the Eagle. They had already overcome many obstacles just to get to this point. But soon they had a new problem. They were running out of fuel.[24]

They hadn't accounted for the extra boost in speed they'd get when separating with Columbia. A burst of air came from undocking (think opening a carbonated drink), and the Eagle had reached a speed of twenty feet per second too fast on descent—over halfway to abort limits. If it increased to thirty-five feet per second above projected, they would have to abort.[25]

The excess speed caused the astronauts to overshoot the landing site the computer was trying to take them to.[26] Neil shifted to manual and steered over the unlandable terrain, but the extra flight time caused them to burn through excess fuel. As they came in for the final approach, an alarm tripped, letting them know they only had sixty seconds' worth of fuel left.[27]

With just thirty seconds of fuel remaining, Aldrin said "Contact light!" (This means at least one of the three sixty-seven-inch probes beneath the spacecraft's four footpads had touched surface, flashing a light on the instrument panel.)[28] Buzz later said that in his estimation they had fifteen seconds of fuel left before they would have had to abort.[29]

Fifteen seconds is all that separated the mission from being successful or a failure. Had they taken just fifteen seconds longer to avoid one more crater, puzzle over the program alarm, deliberate over the right spot to land, or slow themselves down just a bit more, they would have had to cancel the mission, and world history would have turned out completely different.

It's amazing how much can change in fifteen seconds.[30]

The astronauts maintained extreme calm in the midst of intense chaos. How do you tend to respond when you feel the pressures of life?

◑ Do you recall a time where a few key seconds determined the outcome of a major event? What decision was made? How did it change things?

◑ Paul writes, "God will meet all your needs according to the riches of his glory in Christ Jesus" (Philippians 4:19). When is a time that God met your needs with "seconds to spare"? What did those times reveal to you about trusting in him?

DAY TWO: REMEMBER ME

The Bible reveals that Jesus was crucified between two thieves who were being punished for the charges brought against them. We know from Mark's Gospel that at the outset of Jesus' crucifixion, the two thieves had mocked him, crying out for him to prove himself by saving himself and them (see Mark 15:32). Jesus would prove that he was who he said he was, but not by coming off the cross; he would reveal his identity by remaining on it.

Luke's Gospel reveals that one of the two later had a change of heart. Seeing his friend begin to berate Jesus yet again, he told him to knock it off: "We are punished justly, for we are getting what our deeds deserve. But this man has done nothing wrong." Then he turned to Jesus and spoke these familiar words: "Jesus, remember me when you come into your kingdom" (Luke 23:41–42).

It has been said that the common denominator of all people everywhere is that we are all guilty, empty, and scared to die. So, the man must have made the connection: *If this is a king, then he must have a kingdom. If he has a kingdom, perhaps there is a place for me.*

Jesus met his gaze, and the words came quickly. "Truly I tell you, today you will be with me in paradise" (verse 43). Around fifteen seconds was all it took for a man whose life had become a living nightmare to be promised paradise. The man now knew where he was going (paradise), when he would arrive (today), and who would be there to greet him (Jesus).

The afterlife is mysterious and so shadowy and unknown. That's why we fear it. But for this man on this day, he knew all he needed to know. His King would be there to pick him up on the other side. I can just imagine the settled look that must have come over him. The last face he spoke to before he died was also the first person he spoke to in eternity.[31]

Read Luke 23:39–43. What stands out about the two thieves' reactions to Christ?

On the cross, Jesus promised the repentant thief that he would not only be forgiven but that he would also not be forgotten. Why are both important?

What was required on the thief's part for him to receive salvation? What does this reveal about the grace and mercy that God extends to everyone?

DAY THREE: DON'T DELAY

For the thief who asked Jesus to remember him, death by suffocation would have come quickly after his legs were broken. Unable to stand, he would have died in minutes. But we know that when the man closed his eyes here on earth, he came to in heaven. So, what conclusions can we draw from his story—especially if we have questions about our own standing before God?

1. No one is so messed up that they can't be saved. The thief did wrong and deserved what he was experiencing. He didn't have good church attendance. He didn't even get baptized. All he ever did was trust in Jesus as King. But it was enough. As Paul wrote, "Christ has utterly wiped out the damning evidence of broken laws and commandments which always hung over our heads, and has completely annulled it by nailing it over his own head on the cross" (Colossians 2:14, PHILLIPS). In God's eyes, this thief became completely and totally perfect.

2. It is dangerous to delay. You might have less time than you think. A minister once warned his people about the danger of putting off accepting Christ. A man asked him, "What about the thief on the cross?" The minister replied, "Which thief?"[32] That is a frightening question because there were two thieves, not one. And only one made it to paradise.

Doubt and delay are dangerous. So don't delay to tomorrow what God is calling you to do right now! Talk to God in prayer before you end this session. It doesn't have to be polished or pretty. I think prayers are most powerful when they are raw and gritty.

You might feel you are too far from your heavenly Father, that he is an eternity away, but this interaction proves that the one small step of calling out to Jesus is actually a giant leap in reconnecting with your Savior. Calling out to Jesus turned the thief's cross into a launch-pad. And as the final seconds of his life ticked away, the countdown stopped measuring time remaining until death and started measuring time remaining until eternal life.

It's only seconds to paradise.[33]

Read Matthew 20:1–16. What is significant about the fact that the owner paid those who worked in the morning the same as those who only worked later in the day?

Does it seem unfair that someone who has spent their life following their own way can be fully forgiven and saved in the last seconds of their life? Why or why not?

Read Matthew 25:1-13? Who do the wise virgins represent in this parable? What is the danger in delaying and not immediately accepting God's gift of salvation?

DAY FOUR: THE WEIGHT OF GLORY

In January 1962, Neil and Jan Armstrong's daughter, Karen—nicknamed Muffie—died on their sixth wedding anniversary. Her death came after a six-month-long fight with cancer that was discovered after she fell while playing on a playground.[34] In September of that same year, Neil was selected to be an astronaut.[35] At the time, he was a former navy pilot who flew and had a hand in the design of experimental planes for the National Advisory Committee for Aeronautics (NACA), the precursor to NASA. It was all as he dreamed as a child, and now he would go even higher as an astronaut. But it would be while walking through the greatest of griefs.

Yes, Neil had dreams come true. But also nightmares.

Maybe you can relate. Perhaps one thing after another after another has hit you in this life. Sometimes it just feels like too much. In those moments it is normal to question God's goodness or his sovereignty, and even his existence. But in the Bible, we see how the apostle Paul viewed things differently. When he thought about all the things that he had endured in his life, he had this to say:

> Therefore we do not lose heart. Though outwardly we are wasting away, yet inwardly we are being renewed day by day. For our light and momentary troubles are achieving for us an eternal glory that far outweighs them all. So we fix our eyes not on what is seen, but on what is unseen, since what is seen is temporary, but what is unseen is eternal (2 Corinthians 4:16–18).

Paul knew what the trials were doing in him and what was awaiting him when he left this world. This kind of anticipation applies the weight of glory. Weight has everything to do with gravity. Gravity attracts objects together. The greater the mass of an object, the stronger the force of gravity. The smaller the mass, the lesser its gravitational pull.

The moon is smaller than the earth, so on the earth things weigh more, and on the moon they weigh less. A hundred-pound weight here would only weigh about sixteen pounds on the moon, which has one-sixth gravity.[36] When you are standing on the promises of God and not on your circumstances as they presently appear, the mass of your trial gets smaller, and the power of its pull gets weaker. By applying the weight of glory, you put it in perspective.[37]

When have you been tempted to question God's goodness, sovereignty, or existence?

What reasons does Paul provide in 2 Corinthians 4:16–18 for us not to lose heart?

How might the pull of a trial you're going through now grow weaker if you shift the focus from the appearance of circumstances to the promises of God?

DAY FIVE: VIGILANCE REQUIRED

The reward for spiritual progress in one area is usually an attack on a different front. It is easy (and human) to go through one difficult thing and wipe your brow—*phew!*—then let your guard down and be unprepared for the next round. This can quickly sap your morale.

It can be disheartening to feel like you are beginning a new crisis before the old one is barely behind you. This is why we need *vigilance* in this life. And one of the best ways to maintain vigilance and overcome the tendency to put yourself in neutral is to never think you have arrived but stay in drive and maintain your edge. Salvation is not meant to be a finishing line but a starting line. We are supposed to go forth into growth, strength, and power.

If you believe that you've peaked or gone as far as you can go, I dare you to dream deeply and fight with all your heart against disillusionment or the spirit of lethargy. You are meant to move forward. There is more land for you to take. More of your calling for you to fulfill. More character to develop. If you are alive today, it is for a purpose and not an accident.

But there will be opposition. This is the perpetual struggle of following Jesus.

While Jesus wants to light you on fire with the controlled burn of his Holy Spirit igniting power, influence, and love, your adversary, the devil, is working hard to blow you up with trials or crush you with despair. When that doesn't work, he will try to seduce you. And should that fail, he will try to trick you into a spirit of religion and pride. He will never stop trying to tear you down. So, you must never let down your guard.[38]

Read 1 Corinthians 10:12. Where have you experienced victory in one area of life only to let your guard down in another area? What was the result?

Have you considered that many of the obstacles you face aren't random but come from the enemy? How can you be more vigilant against this opposition?

Salvation is not meant to be a finishing line but a starting line. In what ways is God inviting you to move forward now in your calling, relationships, or faith?

For Next Week: Write down any insights or questions you want to discuss at the next group meeting and review chapters 10, 13, and 22 in *The Last Supper on the Moon.*

MISSION ACCOMPLISHED

Here men from the planet Earth first set foot upon the moon. July 1969 AD. We came in peace for all mankind.	**Plaque on the Lunar Module**
Having disarmed the powers and authorities, he made a public spectacle of them, triumphing over them by the cross.	**Colossians 2:15**

WELCOME

The moment had finally arrived. There had been many challenges along the way, both in NASA's trials to get to this point, and in the last-minute obstacles that Neil Armstrong and Buzz Aldrin had been forced to overcome in their descent to the moon. But in the final moments, the call from ground control had been *"go,"* and the astronauts had resolutely pressed ahead in their mission.

Now the team back at ground control waited to receive confirmation that the men had touched down. At last, these words came from Neil: "Houston, Tranquility Base here. The Eagle has landed!" A cheer erupted in the room.[39] Meanwhile, Michael Collins circled the moon in the command module—alone in a way no one in history had ever been. His ship would go around the moon thirty times in twenty hours that Neil and Buzz were on their mission. Each time he circled the moon, he was out of radio transmission for forty-eight minutes.

Back on the moon, Buzz sent a message asking everyone on earth to take the opportunity to pause for a moment, contemplate the events of the past few hours, and give thanks in his or her own way. Following this, he opened a specially prepared packet and took communion—the *Last Supper on the moon.* Six hours and thirty-nine minutes after landing, the two astronauts were ready to go outside. Neil was the first to step out. His foot touched the surface. "That's one small step for a man . . ." he said, "one giant leap for mankind."[40]

The Bible says that Jesus also "resolutely set out for Jerusalem" (Luke 9:51) when the time came for him to fulfill his mission on this earth. He could have aborted the plan at any time, calling down legions of angels to come to his aid, but instead he submitted to his Father's will. He was willing to be crucified on the cross. He willingly hung there for more than six hours—completely alone and separated from the Father.

Jesus did not have to come to this earth. He did not have to give up his life for humanity. No one took his life from him. He *volunteered* for the mission. And through his sacrifice, he has made it possible for us to finally be reconciled with our heavenly Father.

SHARE

Begin your group time by inviting those in the group to share their insights from last week's personal study. Then, to kick things off, discuss one of the following questions:

- Buzz paused to take the Last Supper after landing on the moon. What are some ways that you pause to give thanks to God in your moments of victory?

— *or* —

- The astronauts had a clear definition of success for their mission. Jesus had an equally well-defined mission from the Father. How would you describe it?

READ

Invite someone to read aloud the following passage. Listen for fresh insights as you hear the verses being read, and then discuss the questions that follow.

Therefore, since we are surrounded by such a great cloud of witnesses, let us throw off everything that hinders and the sin that so easily entangles. And let us run with perseverance the race marked out for us, fixing our eyes on Jesus, the pioneer and perfecter of faith. For the joy set before him he endured the cross, scorning its shame, and sat down at the right hand of the throne of God. Consider him who endured such opposition from sinners, so that you will not grow weary and lose heart.

HEBREWS 12:1-3

What is the "race marked out for us?" How are we to run that race?

What did Jesus endure for our sake? What was his motivation?

WATCH

Play the video segment for session four (see the streaming video access provided on the inside front cover). As you and your group watch, use the following outline to record any thoughts or concepts that stand out to you.

The very first thing ever eaten on the moon was bread and wine pointing back to Jesus' sacrifice 2,000 years prior. The first meal ever eaten on the moon was the Last Supper—not an end, but a beginning.

Jesus willingly and voluntarily went with God's plan. We can be tempted to think of Christ's sacrifice as though it were something he did to appease an angry God. But the Bible is clear that Father, Son, and Holy Spirit all together worked hard and all together suffered so that we could be reunited.

When Jesus went to the cross to die for our sins, there was a *go* from the Father, a *go* from the Son, and a *go* from the Holy Spirit. He chose to die for you. He even chose it during his earthly ministry.

Jesus acknowledged there was no other way for us to be saved except by his death. He was willing to pick up the cup and drink it and take the mission the Father had for him. Great power comes when we don't say, "My will be done," but like Jesus, we humbly say to the Father, "Your will be done."

Jesus died on someone else's cross. And not just Barabbas's cross. Jesus died on Levi's cross. He died on your cross. He took what should have been your punishment for sin upon himself. He went to the cross as your substitute.

The word *excruciating* comes from the Latin and literally means "of the cross." It was a fate so bad a word had to be invented to describe it. But that wasn't the worst of it. On top of the physical, emotional, and spiritual toll it would take on someone, Jesus was also completely alone on the cross.

Martin Luther once called the crucifixion the "great exchange," where Jesus was treated like we should be so that we could be treated like he deserves to be. It is staggeringly, absurdly, incomprehensively beyond understanding what Jesus faced on that day. And yet he chose to stay.

The church isn't meant to be a religious experience—a too-righteous-for-my-shirt club where we polish our halos, amen ourselves on how right we are in our theology, and only welcome those who have attained a level of enlightenment like us. It's meant to be messier than that. More broken than that.

DISCUSS

Take a few minutes with your group members to discuss what you just watched and explore these concepts together.

1. Have you ever awaited a final *go* signal from others, as Neil and Buzz did, before you could complete your mission? What was the hardest part of the waiting?

2. Read Isaiah 53:4-6. What does this say about the kind of suffering that awaited Jesus on the cross? What did Jesus understand he would have to endure in order to fulfill God's mission?

3. Jesus said, "I lay down my life—only to take it up again. No one takes it from me, but I lay it down of my own accord" (John 10:17-18). We might be tempted to think that Jesus *had* to die on the cross to appease God, but what does this verse imply? How does it impact you to know that Jesus *willingly* chose to die so you could be saved?

4. Jesus told his followers, "I have come down from heaven not to do my will but to do the will of him who sent me" (John 6:38). What are some ways that you demonstrate that you are submitting to God's will? What does this look like in your life?

5. Read 1 Corinthians 11:23–29. What is the significance of partaking in the Lord's Supper? What should our attitude be when we take communion?

6. Jesus commanded us, "Go into all the world and preach the gospel to all creation" (Mark 16:15). We are all called to carry on his mission of announcing God's plan of salvation to a world that is lost and hurting. How are you currently being an ambassador for his mercy and his agent of rescue for those who feel alienated and forsaken?

R E S P O N D

Briefly review the outline for the video teaching and any notes you took. In the space below, write down the most significant takeaway from this session.

P R A Y

As you close your time together, take a few moments to reflect on the fact that Jesus *willingly* gave up his life on this earth so that you could experience eternal life with him. Thank him for choosing to go through with God's plan for your rescue and ask him to give you the desire to be ambassadors of mercy for others. Use the space below to record any specific prayer requests or praises for the coming week.

Name   Request/Praise

BETWEEN-SESSIONS PERSONAL STUDY

Reflect on the material you covered during this week's group time by engaging in any or all of the following between-session activities. Be sure to read the reflection questions and make a few notes in your guide about the experience. At the start of your next group session, you will have a few minutes to share any insights that you learned.

DAY ONE: ABORT BUTTON

Neil Armstrong and Buzz Aldrin had made it through the program alarms, critically low fuel, craters and boulders, and had finally landed on the moon. Now, the question was stay, no stay.[41] They had to determine if it was safe to remain for the space walk. If anyone at ground control or in the lunar lander determined it wasn't, they would be forced to abort.

Jesus had a similar kind of "abort button" available to him. Twelve legions of angels at the ready. All he had to do was say the word and it would all go away. You can be sure that the devil was playing the same mind games he had in the temptation that preceded Jesus' ministry as Christ reached the halfway point of the crucifixion.

This moment was what Jesus most dreaded. It was all about to be placed on his spiritual account. But it's not just that he paid for it. Jesus didn't just die for you; he died as though he *were* you. Paul put it this way in 2 Corinthians 5:21: "God made him who had no sin to be sin for us, so that in him we might become the righteousness of God." In this moment Jesus was allowed to feel like and be treated as though he had committed every sin he was paying for.

This is why blood ran out of his sweat glands as he prayed, and he asked whether there was any other way. This is what made his chest tighten and caused him to fall head long into the ground and plea with his friends to wake up and pray with him. Just as it is impossible to comprehend the vastness of space and the number of stars, so it is staggeringly, absurdly beyond understanding what distinct horrors he would face when this finally happened.

In the Old Testament, two birds would be brought as a sacrifice for sin. One would be killed, and one would be spared. The blood from the one that died would be placed on the wings of the other, and it would be allowed to fly away. It was spared because it was covered in the blood of the one that died (see Leviticus 14:1–7).

Jesus is the bird that would allow us to fly free.[42]

On the night that Jesus was arrested in the garden, he said to his disciples, "Do you think I cannot call on my Father, and he will at once put at my disposal more than twelve legions of angels?" (Matthew 26:53). Twelve legions would have numbered at least 72,000 angels—all ready to do his bidding at his command. How does this demonstrate the steadfast resolution of Jesus to finish his mission of the cross?

What does Paul say in 2 Corinthians 5:21 happened to Jesus on the cross?

How did the Old Testament sacrificial process involving the two birds foreshadow the ultimate sacrifice of Jesus?

DAY TWO: FORSAKEN BUT NOT FORGOTTEN

Rejection was nothing new for Jesus. But what he felt on the cross was worse than anything that had come before it. He was separated from his Father as far as the east is from the west. This is why he cried out, "My God, my God, why have you forsaken Me?" (Matthew 27:46).

John Stott wrote, "Our sins blotted out the sunshine of his Father's face."[43] Erwin Lutzer added, "Look at these hours on the cross and you are looking into hell: darkness, loneliness, and abandonment by God."[44] It was literally hell on earth. He died so that we might live. And the most amazing thing is he paid this price with joy (see Hebrews 12:2).

But that's not all. If we see this merely as Jesus suffering in life so we would not suffer after death, we miss much of what the cross means. He agonized in torment so we would view the sufferings of this life differently. He experienced darkness so we could have light, distance from God so we could draw near to him, separation so nothing could separate us, shame so we could have honor, and instability so we could have security. And because Jesus was forsaken, we can make sense of the times we have been forsaken.

The actual Greek word for *forsaken* is the same for *abandoned*.[45] You can relate to that, can't you? Maybe you were abandoned by a mom or dad who chose a different family or an addiction instead of you. Perhaps your spouse traded you in for a younger model. Perhaps your skin color has left you marginalized by people who view *white* as a synonym for *normal*. A friend stabbed you in the back. A company rewarded your loyalty with a layoff.

Whatever you have experienced, you can know that Jesus can relate. And he can help you to be something much better than bitter: he can make you an *overcomer*. In Jesus' willingness to be forsaken, you find the secret to healing the wounds you carry from the way people have let you down. His pain becomes your power. You can bring to him every injury and all the trauma and damage you have inside you and entrust it to his nail-pierced hands.[46]

Read 1 Peter 2:24. How does this verse explain the agony that Jesus experienced on the cross? Why did he still choose to go through with his mission?

The actual Greek word for what Jesus experienced on the cross—*forsaken*—is the same word for *abandoned*. When are some times that you have been abandoned in your life? How does it help to know that Jesus experienced this same feeling?

Read Romans 8:37–39. What does it mean to be an *overcomer* in Christ?

DAY THREE: GIVING IS THE KEY TO RECEIVING

On the night Jesus held bread and wine in his hands, he gave one of the most powerful teachings on generosity anywhere in history when he was willing to do what none of his disciples dared—he washed their feet. The disciples were all unwilling to serve each other at the original Last Supper because of the fear that if they humbled themselves and served each other they would be less. In their minds they were only important if they were more important than each other. Jesus taught them a lesson they would never forget when he humbled himself and gave up the perks of being the alpha and took the place of a servant.

John's Gospel tells us how he was able to be "humbled" in this moment, deprived of clout and everything we all think will make us happy. Knowing the Father had given him all things, and that he was going to the Father, Jesus laid aside his mantle and took up a basin (see John 13:3). The key is that Jesus already knew who he was, what he had been given, and where he was going. His identity wasn't up for grabs.

He had conquered his inner space.

The disciples thought, like we do, that they needed to hoard esteem and position and prominence and guard what was theirs because if anyone else's pie slice got bigger, it would make their slice get smaller. Jesus was okay laying his life down on the cross, completely forsaken, because he knew that in so doing, he would be able to take back his life from the grave and with it ours as well. He knew that *giving*, not keeping, is the key to receiving.

Jesus had the power to lay down his life and the power to take it up again. You do too! Follow Jesus' example. Hold on to everything with a light touch. Don't cling to your image or to position or power. When you know who you are and what God has promised, you don't need to be territorial, petty, or defensive. You can have a relaxed confidence and a servant's heart. So, allow Jesus' willingness to fight for you inspire you to fight for the forsaken in your world.[47]

Read John 13:1–9. Jesus knew that God "had put all things under his power" and yet he still determined to humbly wash his disciples' feet. What was Jesus saying to his disciples about *true* power though this action?

When have you been tempted to believe that if someone else's pie slice gets bigger, it means that your slice gets smaller? What are the results of such thinking?

What are some practical ways that you can fight for the forsaken in your world?

DAY FOUR: A JOYFUL REUNION

As they say, in space, no one can hear you scream.[48] While astronaut Michael Collins orbited the earth, no one could hear him at all. As Buzz and Neil descended to the moon in the lunar module Eagle to establish Tranquility Base, he was left in Columbia. For more than twenty hours he was all by himself in a way no one in history had ever been. It must have been eerie.

When I think about the radio silence Michael Collins endured, I can't help but think about Jesus' dark hours on the cross. The Gospels specifically point out the astronomic abnormalities that accompanied the crucifixion. When it should have been its brightest, the sky went black. Noon felt like midnight. It was almost as though the sun was embarrassed to illuminate such a miscarriage of justice. Homicide is the murder of a man. This was that but more; it was *deicide*, the murder of God.

Michael Collins's hours of loneliness ended when the Eagle rose from the moon and rendezvoused with the Columbia in lunar orbit. The prodigal lunar module had come home, and there was a joyous reunion. Here is how Michael described the moment: "The first one through is Buzz. . . . [I] am about to give him a smooch on the forehead . . . but then, embarrassed, I think better of it and grab his hand, and then Neil's. We cavort about a little bit, all smiles and giggles over our success, and then it's back to work as usual."[49]

I get emotional thinking about this scene and thinking about Jesus' reunion with his Father in heaven at the end of his mission. He told his disciples he was going to the Father when he ascended. What a moment that must have been!

But that's not all. All those who have committed their souls into his hands have the promise of life during life and life after death.

This is our living hope! When we shuffle off this mortal coil, we have everything to look forward to. What a reunion awaits us. And I know I won't have Michael's restraint. On that day, it will be all smiles and giggles. But until that day . . . back to work as usual.[50]

Read Matthew 27:45–53. What are some of the "astronomic abnormalities" that took place at Jesus' crucifixion?

The curtain in the temple separated the Holy of Holies— the earthly dwelling place of God's presence—from the rest of the temple where people were permitted to be. Only the high priest was allowed to pass beyond this veil—and only once each year. What is the significance that this curtain was torn in two at Jesus' death?

🌙 What comes to your mind when you think about the reunion you will have in heaven?

DAY FIVE: THE SHEPHERD AND THE GATE

In the Gospel of John, we read how Jesus compared himself to both a gate and a shepherd. "I am the gate for the sheep. . . . I am the gate; whoever enters through me will be saved. . . . I am the good shepherd. The good shepherd lays down his life for the sheep" (John 10:7, 9, 11).

In calling himself a *shepherd*, Jesus was telling us that he is going to take care of us. To have a shepherd looking after you is to have someone completely devoted to you. Endless attention and meticulous care—that is what shepherds give to their sheep. Night and day, shepherds are on call. Just like David chased down a bear and a lion to protect his sheep (see 1 Samuel 17:34–36). That is what Jesus will do for you. You are not just a number to your heavenly Father. Not just one of trillions who have lived. He knows your name, and he wants to have a relationship with you. Every good and bad thing you have faced matters to him.

But what about Jesus calling himself a *gate*? Middle eastern sheep pens in those days would have been circular enclosures with a gap used for entry and no door. The shepherd would use these communal enclosures for the night, and after feeding and watering the flock, would lead them in. He would be the last to enter and would lie down in the opening.[51]

Jesus is a shepherd and a door because in this context the shepherd *is* the door. He would lay down his life for the sheep, metaphorically and literally. To the wolf, and every other predator out there, the message was clear: *To get these sheep you first have to go through me.*

That is what your Savior did for you on the cross. No one took his life from him. He laid it down freely. You are free to enter through the door. You have in-and-out privileges. Come in and out and have good pasture. Listen to his voice. Call his name when you are in trouble. Even if it's been a while and you are ashamed and feel bad. He will put you on his shoulders and sing and rejoice that you have been found (see Luke 15:5). He loves you.[52]

In what ways is Jesus like a *gate*?

In what ways is Jesus like a good shepherd?

What privileges have you been given as a member of Jesus' "flock"?

For Next Week: Write down any insights or questions you want to discuss at the next group meeting and review chapters 8, 19, and 24 in *The Last Supper on the Moon*.

Session Five

THE JOURNEY HOME

I believe that this nation should commit itself to achieving the goal, before this decade is out, of landing a man on the moon and returning him safely to the Earth.

President
John F. Kennedy

Very truly I tell you, whoever hears my word and believes him who sent me has eternal life and will not be judged but has crossed over from death to life.

John 5:24

WELCOME

NASA had finally landed the first two humans on the moon. Neil Armstrong and Buzz Aldrin spent two and a half hours roaming around the surface, checking on their equipment and doing a few experiments for NASA. They also had a phone call with President Richard Nixon and delivered a special object from earth: an American flag.

In the most famous of all the Apollo 11 photos, you can see the flag reflected in Buzz's gold-plated visor—along with Neil and the lunar lander. Buzz appears to almost be inspecting his left wrist. In fact, he was looking at a mission objective checklist when Neil snapped the photo. The men had a laundry list of things to complete before they left the moon.

All too soon, those items had been completed and it was time to depart. The astronauts had a number of switches that needed to be thrown after liftoff. As they went through the checklist, they were horrified to realize the circuit breaker switch that armed the main engine was missing. Buzz had accidently broken it off after hitting it with the corner of his spacesuit, and now there was concern as to how they would fire the engine. Fortunately, the men had a felt-tip pen in the lander, and that was sufficient to place in the slot to activate the switch.

The lunar lander successfully lifted off the moon's surface and soon docked with the command module. The lander was jettisoned, and the crew set a course for home. The final maneuver was to position the command module to enter the earth's atmosphere at a razor-precise angle. After a three-minute communications blackout period, the voice of Neil was heard signaling a successful re-entry. The capsule was recovered. The journey was over!

Jesus likewise had much to accomplish during his earthly ministry—a "laundry list" of items that culminated in his death on the cross. But death could not hold him. Just as Neil and Buzz finished their mission by planting a flag and returning to the command module, so Jesus captured the enemy's flag and returned to his body, the temple that had been torn down, and ascended to heaven from whence he will return to judge the living and the dead.

Jesus' triumph over the grave means that we do not have to fear death, the devil, or anything else that hell can throw at us. It means that we can have God's perfect peace and the assurance that nothing can break off the "switch" that will bring us home. In the words of the apostle Paul, "[Nothing] will be able to separate us from the love of God" (Romans 8:39).

SHARE

Begin your group time by inviting those in the group to share their insights from last week's personal study. Then, to kick things off, discuss one of the following questions:

- What has impressed you most about NASA's successful moon mission? What stands out the most to you about Jesus' successful salvation mission?

— or —

- When was the last time you successfully accomplished an important goal or a mission in your life? How did you celebrate that milestone?

READ

Invite someone to read aloud the following passage. Listen for fresh insights as you hear the verses being read, and then discuss the questions that follow.

[Jesus] died for all, that those who live should no longer live for themselves but for him who died for them and was raised again. So from now on we regard no one from a worldly point of view. Though we once regarded Christ in this way, we do so no longer. Therefore, if anyone is in Christ, the new

creation has come: The old has gone, the new is here! All this is from God, who reconciled us to himself through Christ and gave us the ministry of reconciliation: that God was reconciling the world to himself in Christ, not counting people's sins against them. And he has committed to us the message of reconciliation. We are therefore Christ's ambassadors, as though God were making his appeal through us. We implore you on Christ's behalf: Be reconciled to God. God made him who had no sin to be sin for us, so that in him we might become the righteousness of God.

2 Corinthians 5:15–21

What type of transformation does Paul say takes place when we place our faith in Christ and accept the sacrifice for our sins that he made on our behalf?

What does it mean that Christ "has committed to us the message of reconciliation"? What is our part to play in God's plan to bring redemption to this world?

W A T C H

Play the video segment for session five (see the streaming video access provided on the inside front cover). As you and your group watch, use the following outline to record any thoughts or concepts that stand out to you.

At the end of the Apollo 11 mission, when the astronauts returned to the earth, everyone stood at high alert. Were they alive? Finally, Neil's crackly voice was heard. They had successfully made it back through the atmosphere, back to earth, back to their families. The mission was accomplished.

Jesus had his mind on the "checklist" sewn into his sleeve. He would die for the sins of the world. He would take his life back. His success in his mission gives us the strength to approach ours as well.

When Jesus' last moment arrived, a victorious cry came out of his mouth. Just one word in the Greek *tetelestai,* "It is finished." This was not the normal cry of a victim whimpering and about to die. This was the shout of a victor. This was the noise of triumph.

Jesus' mission was finished in every sense of the word: a servant obeying his master, a work of art being accomplished, a spotless lamb being sacrificed, a debt being paid. We are no longer at war with God. We have been sanctified through the offering of the body of Jesus Christ once for all.

There is perhaps no aspect of conquering inner space more challenging than believing that in the moments when we doubt, in the moments when we worry, in the moments when we wonder—we know that because of the cross, God has forever proven to us that he is madly in love with us.

Heaven is not just a place. It's also a person. It's being with Jesus. And through his spirit, while we live in this world on mission for him, we have his spirit bringing his presence and confidence in us day by day.

Jesus died on the cross, but the truth is that he wasn't *actually* gone. He had just gone home. Out of communication temporarily but not permanently. He would be back. Just as Buzz and Neil had finished their mission by planting a flag near tranquility base, so Jesus had captured the enemy's flag.

Jesus has brought us close to him. He's brought us near. We weren't a people; now we're a people. We weren't citizens; now we're citizens. We were dead; now we're alive. All of this has been made possible through what Jesus did for us—and that can never be overturned.

DISCUSS

Take a few minutes with your group members to discuss what you just watched and explore these concepts together.

1. Neil and Buzz planted an American flag while they were on the surface of the moon. What do you think this act symbolized for themselves and their country at large?

2. Read Colossians 2:13–15. Jesus also symbolically "planted a flag" in his mission. What does Paul say that Jesus accomplished by his death and resurrection?

3. Jesus celebrated a final Passover meal with his disciples that we call the "Last Supper." The traditional Passover meal commemorated how God had saved the Israelites from the angel of death by putting the blood of a lamb on the doorposts of their homes. How did Jesus apply this idea to what he was about to do on the cross? What did he ask the disciples to remember as they ate the bread and drank the wine?

4. On the cross, Jesus proclaimed, "It is finished" (John 19:30). Three words in English but only one in the Greek: *tetelestai*. The word was used in many different sectors of society, but one use was in banking. When a debt had been paid in full, the bankers wrote *tetelestai* on top of the contract. How was the same true as it relates to what Jesus did on the cross?

5. Read Romans 5:6 and 1 John 4:19. There is often no aspect of conquering inner space more challenging than believing God truly loves us in spite of our faults. What do these verses say about God's love? How can we be confident that God loves us?

6. Neil Armstrong and Buzz Aldrin left behind a plaque on the moon that read, in part, "We came in peace for all mankind." Jesus' mission was likewise one of peace. Where in your life right now do you need to especially experience the peace of God?

R E S P O N D

Briefly review the outline for the video teaching and any notes you took. In the space below, write down the most significant takeaway from this session.

P R A Y

As you close this study, take a few moments to thank Jesus for remaining focused on his mission. Acknowledge the price he paid for your salvation, ask him to reveal more about your mission in this season, and praise him for the eternal home he has prepared for you. Use the space below to record any final prayer requests or praises for the coming week.

Name   Request/Praise

_____   _____

_____   _____

_____   _____

_____   _____

_____   _____

_____   _____

_____   _____

Session Five

FINAL PERSONAL STUDY

Reflect on the material that you covered during this week's final group time by engaging in any or all of the following activities. Be sure to read the reflection questions and make a few notes in your guide about the experience. Consider sharing these insights with your group members in the days and weeks following the conclusion of this study.

DAY ONE: IT IS FINISHED

"It is finished" (John 19:30). It's three words in English, but just one in Greek: *tetelestai*. This was not the cry of a victim but the shout of a victor. And as it thundered from Jesus' lips, it reverberated through the corridors of heaven and hell alike, causing angels to rejoice and demons to tremble. Satan's chokehold on humanity had come to an end. No more would man be separated from God. No more would death be able to terrorize.

But what does it mean? *Tetelestai* was actually a common word in that day and used in more than one context. It was used by servants when they finished a job their master gave them. "*Tetelestai*. I did the job you wanted me to do." It was a word used in art. "*Tetelestai*. Nothing more is needed. It's perfect—*voilà!* Quit now." It was a word used by priests. The law required that sheep brought to be sacrificed be without spot or blemish, as you were supposed to give God your best (see Exodus 12:5). When the priests inspected the animal, if it was suitable, they would say, "*Tetelestai*. This sacrifice is without flaw. It is perfect."

One final use of the word was in banking. When you finally paid off something you had financed, they would stamp "*Tetelestai*" on the note. Paid in full. When Jesus said "*tetelestai*," he was saying that your attempt to pay your own bill was now and forevermore unnecessary. His blood became money, and your bill has now been paid.

As the apostle Paul writes, "In him we have redemption through his blood, the forgiveness of sins, in accordance with the riches of God's grace" (Ephesians 1:7). Salvation can't be added to or subtracted from. It's once and for all. A perfect work of art. A masterpiece. The cross is Jesus' last word on your standing before God. It can't be improved upon or altered in any way.[53]

Tetelestai was used by servants, artists, priests, and bankers. How did Jesus' use of this word on the cross take into account all of these meanings and raise it to a new level?

Read Hebrews 10:11–14. The priests in the Old Testament had to repeatedly offer sacrifices to atone for the people's sin. What was different about the sacrifice that Jesus made?

Do you find it difficult to accept the debt has been paid in full for all of your past, present, and even future sins? Why or why not?

DAY TWO: MISSION ACCOMPLISHED

At Mission Control in Houston after Apollo 11 flew, a sentence from John F. Kennedy's May 25, 1961, message to Congress was flashed on the large screen: "I believe that this nation should commit itself to achieving the goal, before this decade is out, of landing a man on the moon and returning him safely to the Earth."[54] An Apollo 11 logo appeared on the NASA screen with the words, "Task Accomplished—July 1969."[55] They had honored their late president in the best way they possibly could—by completing the mission he had sent them on.

Jesus likewise announced that his task on earth had been accomplished when he said, "It is finished" (John 19:30). Guilt? *Finished.* Condemnation? *Finished.* Loneliness? *Finished.* Trying to measure up? *Finished.* Insecurity? *Finished.* Separation? *Finished.*

After his resurrection, Jesus went to great lengths to convey to Peter just how real the shame-destroying power of forgiveness was. Peter had failed and failed big, denying Jesus three times after vowing he would die before betraying him. Peter had said to his friends, "I'm going fishing," which wasn't so much a way to kill time as it was a way of saying, "Party's over." This was his job before Christ. Picking up the fishing game was a way of saying, "There is no way Jesus would want me still on his team."

But Jesus sought him. He cooked a meal over a bed of coals for Peter (see John 21:9). This is significant. Peter denied Jesus over a fire, and so Jesus forgave him over one. He was saying to Peter what our iPhones regularly announce to us: "You have a new memory." He no longer had to be triggered by his self-inflicted trauma whenever smoke wafted into his nostrils.

How tender of Jesus to redeem a fragrance. To overwrite an association. And what Jesus was saying to Peter, he says to you: *When the stone was rolled away on that Easter Sunday, with it I rolled away your shame.* Good night, failure. Good morning, grace.[56]

Read John 21:15–19. When have you, like Peter, felt un-worthy after failing God? How have you seen Jesus re-store you to fellowship with him after these failures?

What most stands out to you in the conversation between Jesus and Peter?

There is a deep human connection between *smell* and *memory*. How has Jesus used an aroma or fragrance to take you back to a particular moment in your story?

DAY THREE: FINAL DESTINATION

When Jesus died on the cross, he paved the way for us to experience eternal life. We can "journey home" to be with him one day, for the cross is our means of salvation. But it's important to emphasize it is the *only* means of salvation, because Jesus is the *only* name that can save.

The Bible says there are two destinations after this life: *heaven* or *hell*. Now, hell is not a subject anyone loves talking about. But we must remember that no one will end up in hell who didn't *choose* to go there. There are two kinds of people: those who say, "Thy will be done" on their way to heaven and those to whom God says, "Thy will be done" on their way to hell. We practically have to crawl over the cross of Jesus, which God planted in our way, in order to get to hell, since he has given us the means to be saved at such precious price.

I read once of a police officer who pulled a man over for an expired registration. The man acknowledged he was in the wrong but had fallen on tough times financially and had no option. The officer listened but, in the end, gave the man a ticket. However, when the officer had driven away, the man realized the ticket in his hand had been wrapped in a hundred-dollar bill. The man was able to use the money to pay the fine and renew his registration.[57]

The officer allowed the full consequences of the law to be felt, but then he absorbed them himself. Only through the reality of hell and the romance of the cross can God be both just and the Justifier of those who believe. God didn't just give humanity a warning, he threw the book against our breaking of his law, but then at the cross he also paid the fine personally.[58]

The cross is still the only means of salvation because Jesus is the only name that can save. Why do you think this is such a divisive statement among people today?

🌙 Read Romans 1:18–25. What does Paul say has been "clearly seen" since the creation of the world? What had God made plain to everyone?

🌙 What ultimately happens to those who choose to reject what God has clearly revealed to humanity and instead follow their own way?

DAY FOUR: REFLECTING THE LIGHT

One of the tasks on the Apollo 11 mission list was for Neil and Buzz to place reflectors on the moon. These reflectors were simple devices, comprised of 100 quartz glass prisms, used as part of an experiment called "lunar laser ranging." Basically, scientists on earth would fire a laser beam up at one of these reflectors and chart how long it took the beam to return back to earth. In this way, they could measure distances between the earth and the moon.[59]

When Jesus was on this earth, he said to his followers, "I am the light of the world" (John 8:12). He was saying that He was God's light come into our world to show us the way, comfort us, and illuminate our lives with his glory. When we have his light, we can see God clearly, can see ourselves clearly, and see each other clearly. When the light dims and we begin to stray from him, everything gets dim. We start to think we look better than we do.

One of the reasons we need to continually read, memorize, meditate on, and apply God's Word is because it gives us access to the light we need. As the psalmist reminds us, "Your word is a lamp for my feet, a light on my path" (Psalm 119:105). The light we find in God's Word will reset the things that are out of whack in our hearts and minds.

When we have God's light within us, we will be able to "reflect" it to others—just like the devices on the moon reflect light back to earth. God has declared war on darkness not by his church shouting at the darkness but by calling us to shine our light into the night. When we reflect like a sliver of a moon instead of the full moon we are meant to be, we limit the hope that God can give to others through us. We fail to reflect his light to our world. Not because the sun isn't bright—but because there is less of ourselves that we are willing to allow God to use.[60]

Read Matthew 5:14–16. Jesus said that he is the light of the world, but he also said that his followers were the light of the world. What did he mean by this?

🌙 What responsibilities do followers of Jesus have to reflect his light to the world?

🌙 What are some of the ways that you are actively reflecting Jesus' light?

DAY FIVE: YOU ARE GO

If you visit the Smithsonian Air and Space Museum, you can stand below the impossibly small, burned Hershey's Kiss command module that Neil, Michael, and Buzz returned home in.[61] The Smithsonian also boasts the Wright brothers' flyer, complete with a dummy lying on the wing, mimicking how it was originally flown in North Carolina.[62]

The two have something in common. Neil brought a piece of the Wright brothers' airplane with him on the Apollo 11 mission—a small bit of cloth from the wing of the *1903 Wright Flyer*, which he carried with him when he stepped out of the lunar module onto the surface of the moon.[63] I love the humility of that gesture.

What it communicates is that we are only here because of what they did back there. Orville and Wilbur flew for the first time in December 1903. They flew one hundred twenty feet. Their flight lasted twelve seconds.[64] Sixty-six years later a piece of their wood-and-fabric flyer would make a quarter-million-mile trip to the moon. Less than one lifetime separated the feeble yet significant first flight from the voyage out of this world.

Here's the point. Jesus said that greater things than he did, you will do (see John 14:12). His death on the cross was not an end; it was just the beginning. He intended his mission to be a Kitty Hawk that would propel you into a life of service, creativity, and beauty the likes of which the world has never seen. The blood, sweat, and tears he paid as he suffered and died for you and me was meant to be a launch point, only the inauguration.

The Last Supper didn't end anything; it began everything. You have a clean slate, a fresh start, and a new heart. No weapon formed against you can prosper (see Isaiah 54:17). The gates of hell can't separate you from the love of God (see Romans 8:38). So, raise the bread and wine and toast the joy of being a child of the kingdom of God, a citizen of heaven.

I want to say to you, as we part, the same thing spoken at 4:15 am on July 16, 1969, when Deke Slayton, Director of Flight Crew Operations, spoke to the crew of Apollo 11 the day of liftoff. He knocked on their bedroom doors and said, "It's a beautiful day; you're go."[65]

It is a beautiful day. And you are *go*.[66]

🌙 Neil brought a piece of the Wright brothers' airplane with him on the Apollo 11 mission to remind himself of the work that others had done to get him there to the moon. Why is it important for us to remember the contributions that others have made in our lives?

Read John 14:11–14. Jesus said that those who believe in him will be able to do even greater things than he has done. What do you think this promise means?

The cross was not an end, but a beginning. Jesus intends for his life, death, and resurrection to propel you into a life of service, creativity, and beauty the likes of which the world has never seen. You are *go*. What will your start of your mission look like?

Next Steps: Well done! You've spent the last five weeks on a journey that took you to the moon and back. As a next step, if you haven't already done so, you may wish to read *The Last Supper on the Moon* from start to finish. We've actually covered less than half of the chapters in this study guide! Above all, I encourage you to continue to fuel your unique mission by spending time in God's Word and with other kindred spirits actively pursuing life with God.

LEADER'S GUIDE

Thank you for your willingness to lead your group through this study! What you have chosen to do is valuable and will make a great difference in the lives of others. The rewards of being a leader are different from those of participating, and we hope that as you lead you will find your own relationship with Christ deepened by this experience.

The Last Supper on the Moon is a five-session study built around video content and small-group interaction. As the group leader, just think of yourself as the host of a dinner party or other gathering. Your job is to take care of your guests by managing all the behind-the-scenes details so that when everyone arrives, they can just enjoy time together.

As the group leader, your role is not necessarily to answer all the questions or reteach the content—the video, book, and study guide will do most of that work. Your job is to guide the experience and cultivate your small group into a kind of teaching community. This will make it a place for members to process, question, and reflect—not necessarily receive more instruction.

Before your first meeting, make sure everyone in the group gets a copy of the study guide. This will keep everyone on the same page and help the process run more smoothly. If some group members are unable to purchase the guide, arrange it so that people can share the resource with other group members. Giving everyone access to all the material will position this study to be as rewarding an experience as possible. Everyone should feel free to write in his or her study guide and bring it to group every week.

SETTING UP THE GROUP

You will need to determine with your small group how long you want to meet each week so that you can plan your time accordingly. Generally, most groups like to meet for either ninety minutes or two hours, so you could use one of the following schedules:

Section	90 Minutes	120 Minutes
Welcome (members arrive and get settled)	10 minutes	15 minutes
Share (discuss one or more of the opening questions for the session)	10 minutes	15 minutes
Read (discuss the questions based on the Scripture reading for the week)	10 minutes	15 minutes
Watch (watch the teaching material together and take notes)	20 minutes	20 minutes
Discuss (discuss the Bible study questions you selected ahead of time)	30 minutes	45 minutes
Respond / Pray (pray together as a group and dismiss)	5 minutes	10 minutes

As the group leader, you'll want to create an environment that encourages sharing and learning. A church sanctuary or formal classroom may not be as ideal as a living room, because those locations can feel formal and less intimate. No matter what setting you choose, provide enough comfortable seating for everyone, and, if possible, arrange the seats in a semicircle so everyone can see the video easily. This will make transition between the video and group conversation more efficient and natural.

Also, try to get to the meeting site early so you can greet participants as they arrive. Simple refreshments create a welcoming atmosphere and can be a wonderful addition to a group study evening. Try to take food and pet allergies into account to make your guests as comfortable as possible. You may also want to consider offering childcare to couples with children who want to attend. Finally, be sure your media technology is working properly. Managing these details up front will make the rest of your group experience flow smoothly and provide a welcoming space in which to engage the content of *The Last Supper on the Moon*.

STARTING THE GROUP TIME

Once everyone has arrived, it's time to begin the group. Here are some simple tips to make your group time healthy, enjoyable, and effective.

First, begin the meeting with a short prayer and remind the group members to put their phones on silent. This is a way to make sure you can all be present with one another and with God. Next, give each person a few minutes to respond to the questions in the "Share" and "Read" sections. This won't require as much time in session one, but beginning in session two, people will need more time to share their insights from their personal studies. Usually, you won't answer the discussion questions yourself, but you should go first with the "Share" and "Read" questions, answering briefly and with a reasonable amount of transparency.

At the end of session one, invite the group members to complete the between-sessions personal studies for that week. Explain that you will be providing some time before the video teaching next week for anyone to share any insights or questions that they have. Let them know sharing is optional, and it's no problem if they can't get to some of the between-sessions activities some weeks. It will still be beneficial for them to hear from the other participants and learn about what they discovered.

LEADING THE DISCUSSION TIME

Now that the group is engaged, it's time to watch the video and respond with some directed small-group discussion. Encourage all the group members to participate in the discussion, but make sure they know they don't have to do so. As the discussion progresses, you may want to follow up with comments such as, "Tell me more about that," or, "Why did you answer that way?" This will allow the group participants to deepen their reflections and invite meaningful sharing in a nonthreatening way.

Note that you have been given multiple questions to use in each session, and you do not have to use them all or even follow them in order. Feel free to pick and choose questions based on either the needs of your group or how the conversation is flowing. Also, don't be afraid of silence. Offering a question and allowing up to thirty seconds of silence is okay.

It allows people space to think about how they want to respond and also gives them time to do so.

As group leader, you are the boundary keeper for your group. Do not let anyone (yourself included) dominate the group time. Keep an eye out for group members who might be tempted to "attack" folks they disagree with or try to "fix" those having struggles. These kinds of behaviors can derail a group's momentum, so they need to be steered in a different direction. Model active listening and encourage everyone in your group to do the same. This will make your group time a safe space and create a positive community.

The group discussion leads to a closing time of individual reflection and prayer. Encourage the participants to take a few moments to review what they've learned during the session and write down their thoughts to the "Respond" section. This will help them cement the big ideas in their minds as you close the session. Conclude by having the participants break into smaller groups of two to three people to pray for one another.

Thank you again for taking the time to lead your group through this exploration of outer space and the mission that Jesus accomplished on this earth. Know that you are making a real difference in the lives of your group members as they seek to conquer their inner space.

ENDNOTES

1. Levi Lusko, *The Last Supper on the Moon* (Nashville, TN: W Publishing, 2021), xxvii–xxviii, xxx.
2. Lusko, *The Last Supper on the Moon,* xl–xli.
3. President John F. Kennedy, address at Rice University in Houston, Texas, on September 12, 1962.
4. Lusko, *Last Supper on the Moon,* xxxi–xxxii.
5. Monica Witt and Jena Rowe, "As Artemis Moves Forward, NASA Picks SpaceX to Land Next Americans on Moon," edited by Katherine Brown, NASA, last updated April 22, 2021, https://www.nasa.gov/press-release/as-artemis-moves-forward-nasa-picks-spacex-to-land-next-americans-on-moon.
6. Lusko, *The Last Supper on the Moon,* xxxii–xxxxiii.
7. Nola Taylor Redd, "Does the Moon Rotate?," Space.com, June 17, 2021, https://www.space.com/24871-does-the-moon-rotate.html.
8. Lusko, *The Last Supper on the Moon,* 2–4, 6, 8.
9. Kermit Zarley, "Did Jesus Carry His Entire Cross?," *Kermit Zarley* (blog), Patheos, March 2, 2015, https://www.patheos. com/blogs/kermitzarley-blog/2015/03/did-jesus-carry-his-entire-cross/; Jean de Climont, *The Mysteries of the Shroud* (2013; reprint, Paris: Assailly Editions, 2016), 39–40; James Stalker, *The Trial and Death of Jesus Christ: A Devotional History of Our Lord's Passion* (London: Hodder & Stoughton, 1905), kindle locations 2572–76, kindle edition; Bill O'Reilly and Martin Dugard, *Killing England* (New York: Henry Holt and Company, 2017), 247, kindle edition.
10. David Terasaka, "Medical Aspects of the Crucifixion of Jesus Christ," *Blue Letter Bible,* 1996, https://www. blueletterbible.org/Comm/terasaka_david/misc/crucify.cfm.
11. Lusko, *The Last Supper on the Moon,* 56–59.
12. Lusko, *The Last Supper on the Moon,* xxxv.
13. Brian Dunbar, "Vehicle Assembly Building," edited by Anna Heiney, NASA, last updated September 23, 2020, https://www.nasa. gov/content/vehicle-assembly-building.
14. Charles Fishman, "This Monster Truck Is One of the Last Pieces of Apollo-Era Space Tech Still in Use," Fast Company, July 2, 2019, https://www.fastcompany.com/90371897/this-monster-truck-is-one-of-the-last-pieces-of-apollo-era-space-tech-still-in-use; Brian Dunbar, "Mobile Launcher," edited by Anna Heiney, NASA, last updated December 21, 2020, https://www.nasa.gov/content/mobile-launcher.
15. Vocabulary.com, s.v., "astronaut," accessed July 14, 2021, https://www.vocabulary.com/dictionary/astronaut; Adam Hadhazy, "How Fast Could Humans Travel Safely Through Space?," BBC Future, August 10, 2015, https://www.bbc.com/future/.
16. Fishman, "This Monster Truck."

17. Lusko, *The Last Supper on the Moon*, 21–22, 24–26.
18. Lusko, *The Last Supper on the Moon*, 28–30.
19. Lusko, *The Last Supper on the Moon*, 32–33.
20. Strong's Concordance, s.v. "5375 *nasa* or *nasah*: to lift, carry, take," Bible Hub, accessed September 15, 2021, https://biblehub.com/hebrew/5375.htm.
21. Lusko, *The Last Supper on the Moon*, 65–66, 69.
22. C. S. Lewis, *Mere Christianity*, revised edition (New York: HarperSanFrancisco, 2001), 175.
23. Lusko, *The Last Supper on the Moon*, 99, 102–106.
24. James Donovan, *Shoot for the Moon: The Space Race and the Extraordinary Voyage of Apollo 11* (New York: Little, Brown and Company, 2019), 511.
25. William Harwood, "The Inside Story of Apollo 11's Nail-Biting Descent to the Surface of the Moon," CBS News, July 15, 2019, https://www.cbsnews.com/news/apollo-11-moon-landing-anniversary-nail-biting-descent-to-the-surface-of-the-moon/.
26. Harwood, "The Inside Story of Apollo 11's Nail-Biting Descent to the Surface of the Moon."
27. Harwood, "The Inside Story of Apollo 11's Nail-Biting Descent to the Surface of the Moon."
28. Eric M. Jones, "The First Lunar Landing," May 10, 2018, in *Apollo 11 Lunar Surface Journal*, edited by Ken Glover, 102:43:16–45:50, https://www.hq.nasa.gov/alsj/a11/a11.landing.html.
29. Buzz Aldrin, "Hear Buzz Aldrin Tell the Story of the First Moon Landing," Science Museum, July 18, 2019, YouTube video, 6:10, https://www.youtube.com/watch?v=9HvG6ZlpLrI.
30. Lusko, *The Last Supper on the Moon*, 119–120.
31. Lusko, *The Last Supper on the Moon*, 122, 126.
32. James Ralph Grant, *The Way of the Cross* (Grand Rapids, MI: Baker Book House, 1963), 44.
33. Lusko, *The Last Supper on the Moon*, 129–131.
34. James Donovan, *Shoot for the Moon: The Space Race and the Extraordinary Voyage of Apollo 11* (New York: Little, Brown and Company, 2019), 183.
35. Amy Shira Teitel, "Before the Moon: The Early Exploits of Neil Armstrong," BBC News, September 22, 2015, https://www.bbc.com/news/science-environment-34170799.
36. "Here Are 13 Nuggets of Lunar Knowledge," *National Geographic*, July 16, 2004, https://www.nationalgeographic.com/science/article/moon-facts.
37. Lusko, *The Last Supper on the Moon*, 154–155, 159–160.
38. Lusko, *The Last Supper on the Moon*, 197–199, 202.
39. "Apollo Expeditions to the Moon," chapter 11.4, NASA, https://history.nasa.gov/SP-350/ch-11-4.html.
40. "Fifty Years Ago: One Small Step, One Giant Leap," NASA, https://www.nasa.gov/feature/50-years-ago-one-small-step-one-giant-leap.
41. Eric M. Jones, "The First Lunar Landing," May 10, 2018, in *Apollo 11 Lunar Surface Journal*, edited by Ken Glover, MP3 audio clip from the network controller's loop, 33:04, 37:40.

42. Lusko, *The Last Supper on the Moon*, 207, 209–210.
43. John R. W. Stott, *The Cross of Christ, 20th anniversary edition* (Downers Grove, IL: InterVarsity Press, 2006), 81.
44. Erwin W. Lutzer, *Cries from the Cross: A Journey into the Heart of Jesus* (Chicago: Moody Publishers, 2002), 98.
45. Strong's Concordance, s.v. "1459 *egkataleipó*: to leave behind, desert, abandon," Bible Hub, accessed October 12, 2021, https://biblehub.com/greek/1459.htm.
46. Lusko, *The Last Supper on the Moon*, 212–214.
47. Lusko, *The Last Supper on the Moon*, 216–217.
48. *Alien*, directed by Ridley Scott (Brandywine Productions, 1979).
49. Michael Collins, *Carrying the Fire: An Astronaut's Journey* (1974; reprint, New York: First Cooper Square Press, 2001), 419.
50. Lusko, *The Last Supper on the Moon*, 329, 333–334, 342–343.
51. "Ancient Sheep Fold," Bible History, accessed August 4, 2021, https://www.bible-history.com/sketches/ancient/sheep-fold.html.
52. Lusko, *The Last Supper on the Moon*, 168–170.
53. Lusko, *The Last Supper on the Moon*, 292–293, 296–297.
54. John F. Kennedy, "Address to Joint Session of Congress" (speech, United States Capitol, Washington, DC, May 25, 1961), Space.com, https://www.space. com/11772-president-kennedy-historic-speech-moon-space.html.
55. NASA's Johnson Space Center (@NASA_ Johnson), "50 years ago, #Apollo11 astronauts splashed down in the Pacific Ocean," Twitter, July 24, 2019, https://twitter.com/nasa_johnson/status/1154029751268282368.
56. Lusko, *The Last Supper on the Moon*, 298–299.
57. "Texas Police Officer Wraps $100 Bill in Traffic Ticket," Officer.com, December 12, 2012, https://www.officer. com/command-hq/technology/traffic/news/10841300/plano-texas-police-officer-wraps-100-bill-inside-traffic-ticket; J. D. Miles, "Plano Police Officer Wraps $100 Bill in Traffic Ticket," CBSN Dallas–Ft. Worth, December 11, 2012, https://dfw.cbslocal.com/2012/12/11/plano-police-officer-wraps-100-bill-in-traffic-ticket/.
58. Lusko, *The Last Supper on the Moon*, 126–128.
59. "The Apollo Experiment That Keeps on Giving," NASA Jet Propulsion Laboratory, accessed October 12, 2021, https://www.jpl.nasa.gov/news/the-apollo-experiment-that-keeps-on-giving.
60. Lusko, *The Last Supper on the Moon*, 140, 144.
61. "Apollo 11 Command Module Columbia," Smithsonian National Air and Space Museum, accessed August 26, 2021, https://airandspace.si.edu/collection-objects/command-module-apollo-11/nasm_A19700102000.
62. "1903 Wright Flyer," Smithsonian National Air and Space Museum, accessed August 13, 2021, https://airandspace.si.edu/collection-objects/1903-wright-flyer/nasm_A19610048000.
63. David McCullough, *The Wright Brothers* (New York: Simon & Schuster Paperbacks, 2015), 262.
64. "1903 Wright Flyer," Smithsonian National Air and Space Museum.
65. James Donovan, *Shoot for the Moon: The Space Race and the Extraordinary Voyage of Apollo 11* (New York: Little, Brown, 2019), 3; Jennifer Lu, "Deke Slayton's Moon Shot: How the Man Who Picked the Apollo 11 Crew Finally Got to

Fly," *La Crosse Tribune*, July 15, 2019, https://lacrossetribune.com/news/local/deke-slaytons-moon-shot-how-the-man-who-picked-the-apollo-11-crew-finally-got/article_b283eb03-1f16-5da4-9949-1a066febd445. html.

66. Lusko, *The Last Supper on the Moon*, 367–368, 375.

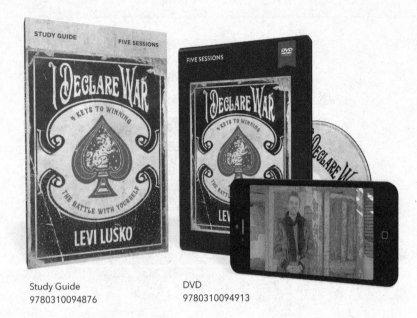

Also available from Levi Lusko

Study Guide
9780310118916

DVD with
Free Streaming Access
9780310118930

Have you ever looked back on a comment, response, or action you took and asked yourself, "Why did I do that?" Do you ever feel as if you are losing the battle to control your thoughts? Most likely you've tried to change in the past, but your struggles still persist.

Come to terms with the reality of this battle and the weapons that God has given you to engage in the fight. In the end, you will find it is not enough to just participate in the war—you have to be an active combatant and know the tactics of your enemy.

Available now at your favorite bookstore,
or streaming video on StudyGateway.com.

Study Books of the Bible with Trusted Pastors

The 40 Days Through the Book series has been designed to help believers in Christ more actively engage with God's Word. Each study in the series encourages participants to read through one book in the New Testament at least once during the course of 40 days and provides them with:

- A clear understanding of the background and culture in which the book was written,

- Insights into key passages of Scripture, and

- Clear applications and takeaways from the particular book that participants can apply to their lives.

H HarperChristian Resources

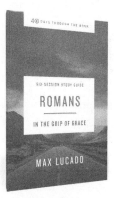

ROMANS
In the Grip of Grace

Max Lucado

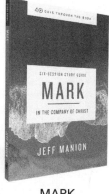

MARK
In the Company of Christ

Jeff Manion

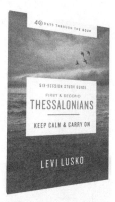

THESSALONIANS
Keep Calm and Carry On

Levi Lusko

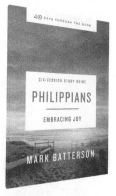

PHILIPPIANS
Embracing Joy

Mark Batterson

COMING SOON!

EPHESIANS
Life in God's Diverse Family

Derwin Gray

Available November 2021

New Video Study for Your Church or Small Group

Lysa is passionate about coming alongside readers on their own journeys of forgiveness, whether the deepest pain comes from years ago or is still happening today. If you've enjoyed this book, now you can go deeper with the companion video Bible study and journal!

In the six-session study, Lysa TerKeurst helps you apply the principles in *Forgiving What You Can't Forget* to your life. The study guide includes video notes, group discussion questions, and personal study and reflection materials for in between sessions. *The Forgiveness Journal* is a unique interactive companion that includes journaling prompts for personal processing, along with space to write and beautiful color photos of the places where Lysa worked through her own healing.

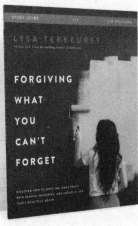

Journal
9781400224388

Study Guide
9780310104865

DVD with
Free Streaming Access
9780310104889

Available now at your favorite bookstore,
or streaming video on StudyGateway.com.

What do you do when God's timing seems questionable, His lack of intervention hurtful, and His promises doubtful?

Lysa invites you into her own journey of faith and, with fresh biblical insight, grit, and vulnerability, helps you to see your life in the context of God's bigger story. The six-session video series is perfect for your Bible study, book club, small group, or individual use. Join Lysa TerKeurst as she unpacks the Scriptures even more fully and helps apply the teaching to your specific situations. The study guide includes video notes, group discussion questions, and activities for groups, plus personal study and reflection materials for in-between sessions.

ItsNotSupposedToBeThatWay.com
or wherever books are sold
Streaming video on StudyGateway.com

New Video Study for Your Church or Small Group

Lysa is passionate about coming alongside readers on their own journeys of forgiveness, whether the deepest pain comes from years ago or is still happening today. If you've enjoyed this book, now you can go deeper with the companion video Bible study and journal!

In the six-session study, Lysa TerKeurst helps you apply the principles in *Forgiving What You Can't Forget* to your life. The study guide includes video notes, group discussion questions, and personal study and reflection materials for in between sessions. *The Forgiveness Journal* is a unique interactive companion that includes journaling prompts for personal processing, along with space to write and beautiful color photos of the places where Lysa worked through her own healing.

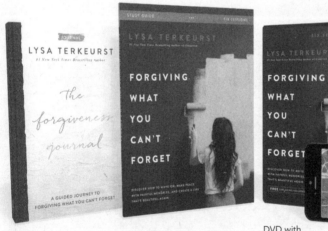

Journal
9781400224388

Study Guide
9780310104865

DVD with
Free Streaming Access
9780310104889

Available now at your favorite bookstore,
or streaming video on StudyGateway.com.

It's Not the Height
of the Giant
. . . but the Size of
Our God

Explore the principles in *Goliath Must Fall* with your small group through this six-session video-based study. Each week, pastor Louie Giglio will provide practical steps and biblical principles for how you and your group can defeat the "giants" in your lives like fear, rejection, comfort, anger, or addiction. Includes discussion questions, Bible exploration, and personal study materials for in between sessions.

Available now at your favorite bookstore,
or streaming video on StudyGateway.com.

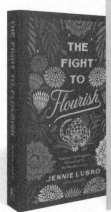